CLAY CREATION
workshop

100+ Projects to Make with Air-Dry Clay

maureen carlson

IMPACT
CINCINNATI, OHIO
www.impact-books.com

Contents

1 CLOTHES AND PEOPLE

2 PETS

3 FROM THE KITCHEN

4 HAIR AND SALON

5 BEADS, BAUBLES AND BLING

6 RECREATION

7 ZOO ANIMALS

8 MORE CUTE ANIMALS

9 JUST A FEW MORE...

Note

The clay that is used for the projects in this book is a super soft, lightweight, air dry clay. There are many brands on the market, including, among others, Cloud Clay, Creatology Air Dry Clay and Model Magic. Oven-baked polymer clay, kiln-fired clays and heavier, wetter air dry clays are not appropriate for most of the projects in this book.

These lightweight, air dry clays are easy to work with, providing hours of entertainment and experience in making 3-D art. They are colorful, nearly mess-free and require very little in the way of equipment or tools.

The packages may vary in consistency depending on the brand and whether the package is airtight. Since the clay begins to dry upon contact with air, it is important to keep the clay protected in airtight containers or bags. Generally it dries to the touch in 24 hours. If the clay is too soft, leave it exposed to the air until it starts to dry a bit.

Usually the clay does not stick to hands, though it sticks very easily to itself. Provide yourself with a suitable work area because some of the colors may stain hands or work surfaces. Washing with soap and water will remove most stains.

Tips and Tricks for Using Super Lightweight, Air Dry Clay

Inside each package of lightweight, air dry clay is a whole world full of creations. It's up to you to imagine it all into being. But you'll have help. Lots of help. This book is full of tips, tricks and ideas to help you do just that. Ready to start?

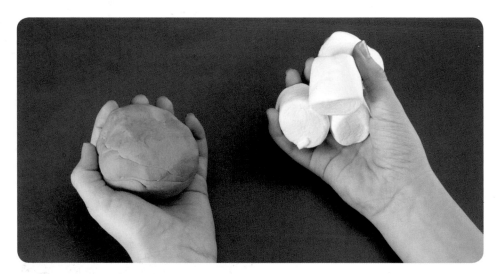

USE THE RIGHT CLAY

Does the clay that you are using feel light, like a marshmallow? Are the words **air dry** printed somewhere on the package? If so, then you probably have clay that will work for making these animals.

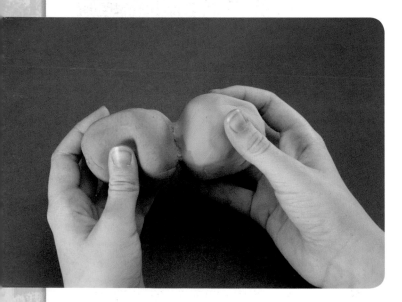

KEEP IT SEPARATED

If you want one piece of clay to stick to another, just touch them together. It's that easy. If you don't want them to stick, keep the pieces separated.

MIX IT UP

Create striped clay by twisting two or more colors together. Make solid colors by twisting the colors together, rolling and folding, then twisting again.

PROP IT

Help your creations keep their shape by propping them up until they are completely dry. This won't matter for some pieces, but an arm that you want to stay up in the air or those wings that are posed for lift off will droop if not propped in place.

KEEP IT COVERED

Clay that is dried out doesn't stick to itself very well. And it doesn't roll into a smooth ball or shape. To keep it fresh, store it in an airtight container or bag. Seal the container every time you use the clay.

KEEP PROJECT COLORS TOGETHER

Put all of the colors that you'll use for a project into one gallon-sized bag. If the colors keep sticking together, keep them separate by wrapping each in a piece of plastic wrap. Flatten the bag to press out the air, then fold over the top if you'll be using it right away. Remember to tightly close the bag when you're done with the project so you can use the clay another time.

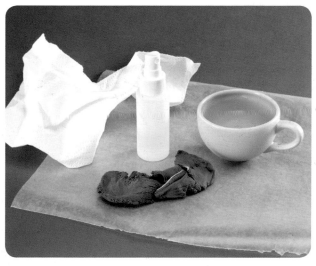

REVIVE DRIED-OUT CLAY

If your clay dries out, try folding and twisting it to see if it becomes workable. Still too dry? Place it in a plastic bag and sprinkle a little bit of water on it. Too much water will make it very sticky. Leave the clay in the bag for a few minutes, then twist and mix it to see if it's workable again. If your clay is very dry, you may have to add more water and let it rest even longer. Completely dried-out clay usually cannot be revived, so remember to keep it covered!

Tools You Can Use

Make yourself an art supply box. Decorate the outside if you like and put your favorite art supplies and tools in it. That way you'll always know where they are, and they'll be there when you're ready to create.

You don't have to go out and buy all new tools. Look around and see what you already have that might work. Here are some suggestions.

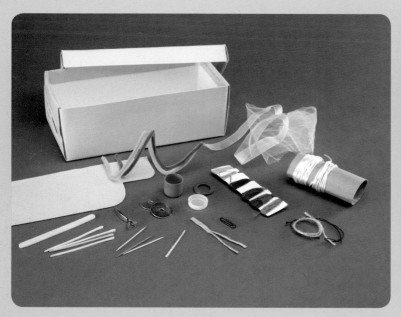

FILL YOUR TOOLBOX

Barbecue skewers	Glue stick	Scissors
Barrettes	Knitting needles	Shoe boxes
Beads	Old toothbrushes	Straws
Blocks	Paintbrushes	Twist ties
Bottle caps	Paper	Washers or weights
Craft sticks	Paper clips	Watercolor markers
Dull knife	Plastic bags	Watercolor paint
Flat and round toothpicks	Plastic wrap	Wax paper
Glitter glue	Ruler	White glue that dries clear

A Quick Lesson in Making Faces Using Tools From Your Toolbox

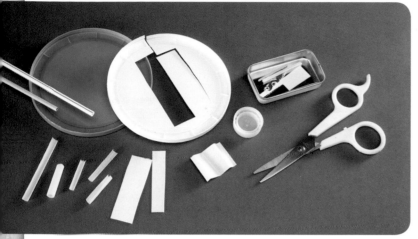

HOMEMADE TOOLS

Not all art supplies need to be purchased. Toilet paper and paper towel tubes, boxes and scrap paper can be rescued from the trash bin. Watch for small jars and cans in the trash and save them to use as handy containers, but make sure they don't have sharp edges and are well rinsed. Some of my favorite tools are ones that I make from drinking straws and plastic lids.

Pieces of a straw can be used for making curved lines. To make straw tools, cut drinking straws in sections, then cut them again lengthwise.

Pieces cut from a plastic lid also make great cutting tools. Make them in different sizes so you'll have some choices. Bend some pieces to make wavy lines or long curved lines.

A QUICK LESSON IN MAKING MOUTHS

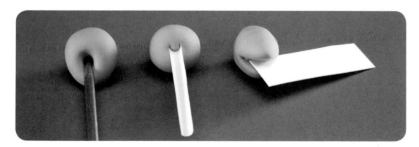

USE THE BEST TOOL FOR THAT SHAPE
A knitting needle or round tool might work best for making a round mouth, while a cut straw tool is a quick and easy way to make a grinning smile. Straight lines are easily made with a piece of plastic that you cut from a plastic lid.

USING THE STRAW
To use a straw tool to make small, curved lines, pinch the edges together before pressing. It works great for making the doubled curve of a cat's mouth.

HOW TO MAKE MOUTHS WITH PERSONALITY
To give more personality to a mouth, press in the corners with a rounded tool such as this knitting needle. It will turn a little grin into a bigger smile.

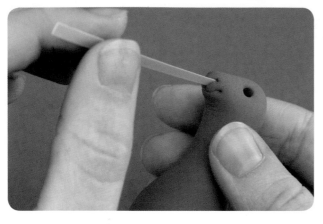

MAKE A NOSE

Use a tiny piece of cut plastic to make the lines for a nose.

USE BEADS FOR EYES

Pony beads can become eyes or glasses, depending on how you use them. To make eyes, press the bead in place, then drop a tiny clay ball into the middle of each bead. Poke the center with a toothpick.

MAKE GLASSES

To make glasses, press a tiny roll of clay between the beads. This will also cover up cracks, which sometimes happen when the clay dries.

USE A DRINKING STRAW TOOL FOR MOUTHS

To make simple mouths, press a small ball of pink clay where the mouth will be. Then use a piece of cut drinking straw to press in a curved line. It's quick and easy!

To form the straw tools, cut a straw into short sections, then cut each section in half, lengthwise. Trim some pieces to create a narrow tool and some to make wider ones.

USE GLUE AND TOOTHPICKS

Use glue and short pieces of toothpick to help hold shoes onto legs and hands onto sleeves. It isn't always necessary, but sometimes these small pieces dry out while you're working on them. They may seem to stick, but will fall apart easily once they're dry.

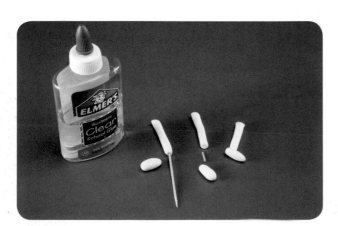

How to Make Basic Shapes

All of the clay projects in this book begin with a ball shape because it's the easiest shape to make and the most useful. It's also the fastest way to get the clay smooth and to get the wrinkles out.

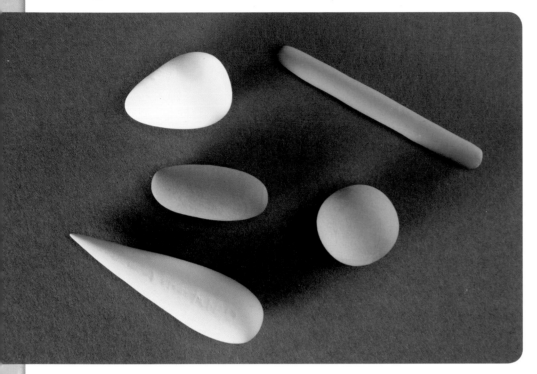

When making shapes, first make a ball. Then you can quickly turn the ball into a teardrop, an oval, an egg or a rope.

THE BALL

All of the animals in this book start with one or more of six basic shapes. Learn to make a ball, an oval, an egg, a teardrop, a drumstick and a rope and you'll be able to make all of the animals in this book. Of course, not all six are used in every animal. However, learning to make these shapes will help in creating that special combination of shapes that makes each animal unique. To illustrate this, let's see what would happen if we used just one shape to make an animal.

A REGULAR BALL

A ball is the easiest shape to learn to make. Rolling a ball is the fastest way to get the clay smooth and to get the wrinkles out. Once you make a ball, you can turn it into any of the other shapes.

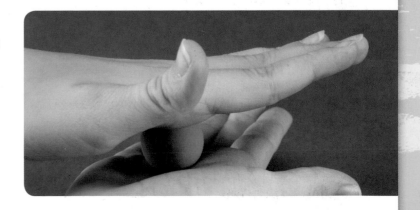

ODD BALLS
Rolling a ball of clay seems simple enough—just rotate your hands in a circle as you press lightly against the clay. But if you press too hard, you may get a disk or a football shape. If you press too lightly, or if the clay is too dry, you won't be able to get the wrinkles out.

THE BALL DOG
This clay character's head, body, legs, eyes, ears and nose are all made from ball shapes.

THE OVAL

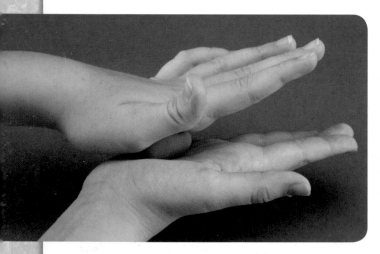

MAKE AN OVAL SHAPE
To make an oval shape, start with a ball, then slide your hands back and forth just a few times. Make sure to stop before it turns into a rope.

THE OVAL DOG
This clay character's entire body is made up of oval shapes.

THE ROPE

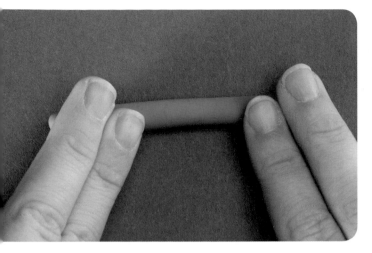

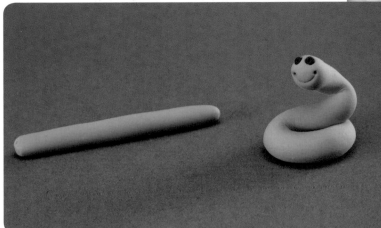

MAKE A LENGTH OF ROPE

To make a long rope, first make a ball, then an oval. Keep rolling, and it will turn into a rope. To make it longer, lay it on the table and keep rolling, but move your hands away from the center as you roll. Don't push down too hard. Roll and stretch the clay into a long, skinny rope.

THE ROPE WORM

This clay character is made up of one long, twisted rope shape.

THE EGG

MAKE AN EGG

To make an egg shape, hold a ball in your cupped hands. Be sure that your little fingers and the sides of your hands are touching and your thumbs are pointed out. Roll your hands back and forth, pressing lightly on the ball. Roll just long enough for the ball to turn into an egg shape.

THE EGG-EARED RABBIT

This clay character is made up of egg shapes.

THE DRUMSTICK

MAKE A DRUMSTICK

To make a drumstick shape, start with a ball, then make an egg. Roll your finger just below the small part of the egg. This creates an indentation so the clay looks like a chicken drumstick. To make the shape more exaggerated, just keep rolling.

THE DRUMSTICK DOG

This clay character is mostly made up of drumstick shapes! As you start making the animals in this book, you'll use the drumstick shape over and over again to make animal heads and body parts.

THE TEARDROP

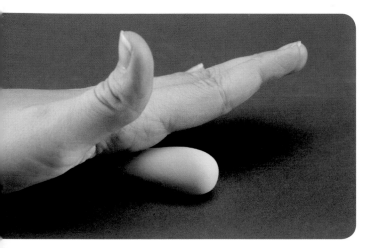

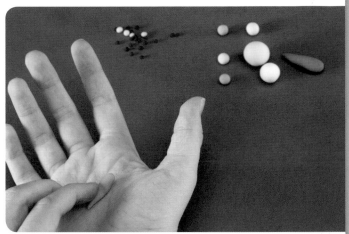

MAKE A TEARDROP

To make a teardrop shape, place a ball on the table. Lay your hand over it with your thumb up in the air and the other side of your hand on the table. Your hand will be tilted. Roll back and forth, pressing lightly on the ball. The side of the ball that is under your hand will become long and pointed like a carrot.

MAKING LITTLE SHAPES FOR TEETH, NOSES AND EYEBALLS

Some shapes are easier to use if you make them ahead of time and let them dry before pushing them into the clay. Make a stash of little shapes by rolling them in the palm of your hand, using one finger to form the shape. Then keep these on hand, ready for when you need them.

MAKE A POINTY-EARED RODENT

This clay character is made up of teardrop shapes.

Clay Characters: Basic Body Building

Before we begin accessorizing our clay characters, we need to actually make them. Here are a few basic steps to building your clay characters from some of the techniques you've already learned.

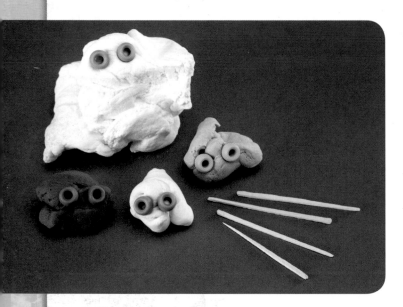

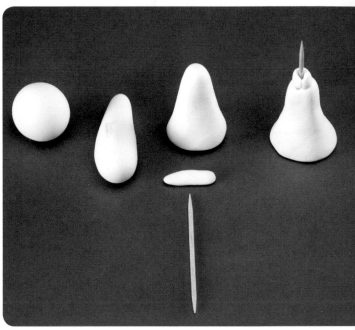

GATHER YOUR SUPPLIES
Beads or colored clay for eyes, white clay, skin tone colored clay and toothpicks.

MAKE THE DRESSES
1. Make a ball, then shape it into an egg.
2. Flatten the large end of the egg to make a cone shape.
3. Stretch out the bottom a bit to make a skirt.
4. Add a toothpick "backbone" to hold the head in place. Use a strip of white clay for the neck. The size of the cone depends on how big you want your girls to be.

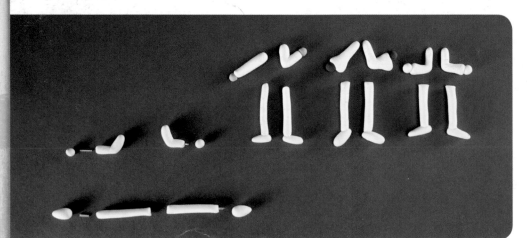

MAKE ARMS AND LEGS
For the legs, cut one rope in half and use egg shapes for the shoes. Be creative with how you want to make the arms and use a ball for each hand. If you want the girls to sit on a bench, bend the legs at the knees.

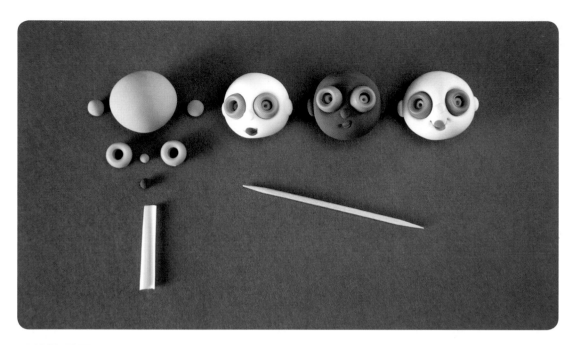

MAKE THE HEADS

Experiment with using different sizes of balls for the
mouth, nose and ears.

ASSEMBLE THE GIRLS

1. Press the legs to the bottom of the dress.
2. Press on the arms.
3. Add the head last.
4. Let the girls dry overnight before adding hair, because wet clay can easily be
smashed out of shape.

1 CLOTHES AND PEOPLE

Designing Clothes

In this chapter we're going to explore different ways of designing fashionable clothing for your clay characters.

HOW TO USE WATERCOLOR MARKERS TO MAKE PATTERNS

Watercolor markers work great on air dry clay if you follow these rules:

1. Let the clay dry before using the markers. If the figures haven't hardened, they will easily be broken or bent out of shape as you concentrate on painting. Wet clay may also cause the watercolor to bleed or run.
2. Be sure that your hands are dry. Wet hands will pick up color from the designs and leave smudges wherever you touch the clay.

ADD PATTERNS

Use markers to make various designs on the girls' outfits. Make stripes, add dots or create wavy lines. Add as many other patterns that you can think of. If you need inspiration, just look at your own clothes to get ideas.

ADD FLOWERS

If you're an avid gardener, you might want to try a flower pattern. These flowers are simple loops with a dot in the center.

SHOE DESIGNS

Shoes don't have to be plain. Add marks for shoelaces or buttons. If the shoes pop off while you're working, use glue to re-attach them. When you make the shoes, remember to use glue and a piece of broken toothpick to fasten them in place.

Designing Clothes Using Colored Clay

I like bright rainbow colors so instead of starting with white clay, let's begin with brightly colored clay to make a few different outfits.

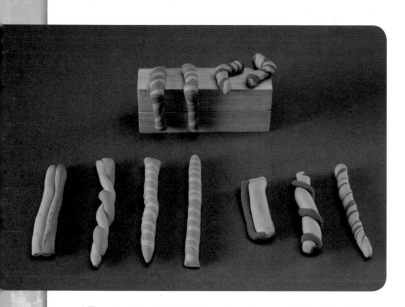

1 HOW TO MAKE COLORFUL CLAY STRIPES

These legs and arms were made by twisting together two colors of clay. Twist, then roll to smooth. Twist and roll again. When you like it, stop. Cut the length that you need and shape the legs and arms.

2 MAKE THE BODY PARTS

These clothes look way more complicated now than they did when the character was dressed all in white. But the shapes are the same, it's just the colors that are different. Her dress is still an egg shape that was flattened on the big end into a cone shape. Her arms are the same shape as before, but now they look like striped sleeves. She appears to be wearing striped leggings. Her shoes are still eggs, and her hands are still balls. Her neck, instead of being the color of her skin, is one of the colors from her leggings.

1 HOW TO MAKE A VEST

Let's make an orange vest to match the orange shoes. Begin with a ball of clay that is about the size of her head. Notice that this character's head isn't on yet. That's because it's easier to dress characters if you leave the head until last. Roll the ball into a rope shape, then flatten it to create a rectangle. Make it about as thick as a banana peel.

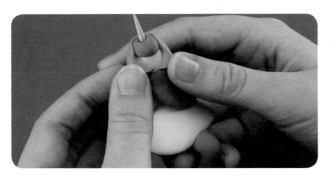

2 FINISHING TOUCHES OF THE VEST

Wrap the rectangle around the top of the dress, overlapping it in front. Turn down the upper corners to create a collar. The dress and legs should already be dry and hard when you add the vest. If yours isn't hard, add the vest without picking the rest of the clay body up.

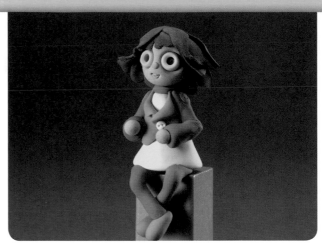

3 ARMS AND LEGS

Add the arms and head. Notice that I added clay buttons to the arms, it's important to embelish where you see fit.

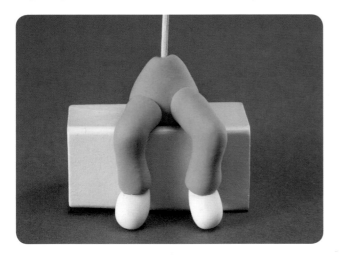

1 MAKE PANTS

To make pants, roll an egg that is about half as tall as one you would make for a dress. Make the legs and press them to the front of the egg. Add a toothpick backbone.

2 MAKE A SHIRT

To make this marbled shirt, mix several colors of clay together until they are swirled. Stop before the colors turn muddy. Roll a ball and then an egg shape. Flatten it into a cone shape.

3 MAKE MORE SPACE

Press your fingers into the center of the cone to create a hollow space. Stretch the edges to make them thinner.

4 ADD THE BODY PARTS

Press the top over the pants and over the toothpick. If the top won't go down far enough, use your thumbs to create a larger hole in the bottom of the cone. Then add the neck, arms and head.

Making Accessories: Purses, Boots and Bows

Every girl has their favorite pair of boots and clay girls are no different, so let's make a variety of accessories. You could make enough things to fill up a fashion boutique. Or, if you'd rather, make just one or two for the girls to share. Either way, here are a few ideas to get you started.

PURSES

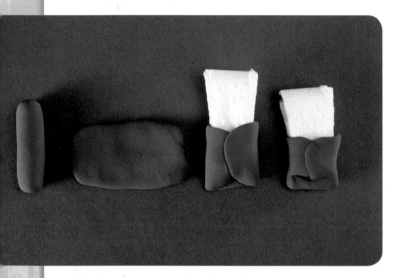

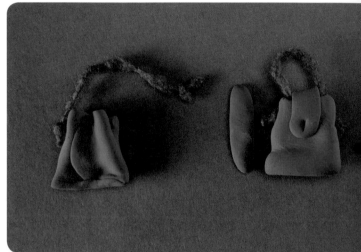

1 HOW TO MAKE A PURSE

Roll a rope that is slightly taller and half as wide as you want the finished purse to be. Flatten it into a rectangle about the thickness of a banana peel. Then roll up a piece of paper towel to fit into the center of the purse. Tape the paper edges to hold them in place. Wrap the clay rectangle around the paper towel and overlap the clay edges and press together. Fold up the bottom.

2 ADD A HANDLE

There are a number of ways to finish the purse. One way is to remove the paper towel, then press the top edges together to create wrinkles. Knot the ends of a short piece of string. Press the knots either into the top of the purse or between two folds of clay. Press the clay around the knots to hold the string in place. Let dry.

3 ADD A FLAP AND SOME BLING

To add a flap, flatten a short rope. Press the flap over the top of the purse. Add a clay button. Then use glitter glue to add initials, buttons or designs.

BOOTS

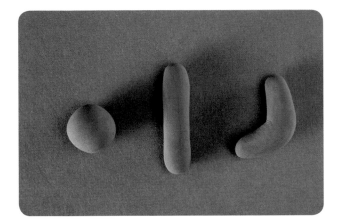

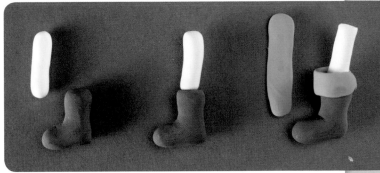

1 **HOW TO MAKE BOOTS**
Roll a ball and then a rope. Decide how tall and how big you want the boots to be. Bend the boots at the heel. Trim the top if it's too long.

2 **MAKE THE LEG AND THE CUFF**
Use your fingers to shape the heel of the boot. Roll a rope that's the color of the leg, socks, leggings or pants. Press the leg to the top of the boot. Wrap a flattened piece of clay around the top of the boot to create a cuff. Then repeat these steps for the other leg.

BOWS

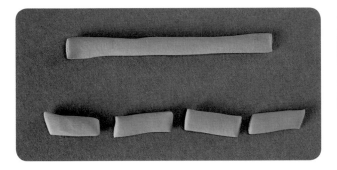

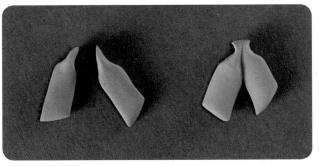

1 **HOW TO MAKE A BOW**
From a flattened piece of rope, cut four short strips.

2 **MAKE THE TAILS**
To create the tails, pinch the tops of the two strips of clay into a point. Press these two together.

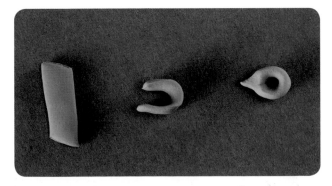

3 **MAKE THE LOOPS**
To create the rounded part, fold the other two strips into a circle shape. Pinch together the part where the ends meet.

4 **FINISH THE BOW**
To finish the bow, use a toothpick to pick up and press the circle parts to the tops of the tails.

How to Change Your Clay Characters' Clothes

There are so many ideas for making clothes that you might not know where to start. So let's begin with making interchangeable parts. If you haven't noticed, then it's good to note that the heads are removable. This allows you to be able to design several bodies for each character.

Now let's focus on making the arms removable as well.

1 HOW TO MAKE REMOVABLE ARMS

In this photo, you see one clay character in a red dress with striped sleeves. Her other outfit is all white, but the arms aren't attached. Both outfits were built the same way but with different colors and shapes.

Notice that there is an extra ball of clay at each shoulder. These were added to widen the shoulders. A piece of flat toothpick was pressed all the way through the shoulders and shoulder balls. There is a hole for the toothpick at the top of each arm.

2 SWITCH IT UP

After all the pieces are thoroughly dry, you can switch the head and arms to make it look like she has four different outfits. Because the arms and head move, you can also position her doing different things or looking in different directions.

Here is a finished outfit. Notice that there are layers of clothes, combining everything that you have learned to make in this chapter.

THE BASIC STEPS FOR MAKING A MULTILAYERED CLAY OUTFIT

1. Legs: Make the striped legs.

2. Boots: Make boots and add them to the legs. The bows were made out of colored string.

3. Dress: Make the cone-shaped dress. Press the dress over the legs and add a toothpick backbone and neck.

4. Vest: Make a vest and wrap it around the top of the dress.

5. Jacket: Make the jacket, which is just like the vest but wider and longer. Add shoulder balls. Press a piece of flat toothpick through the shoulders.

6. Arms: Make the hands and arms. Poke a hole for the toothpick at the top of each arm. Then let the arms and body dry.

7. Head: Make the head. Add hair. Let the head dry.

8. Hat: Make a hat to fit the head. Let dry.

9. Purse: Make a purse. Let dry.

10. Add bling: Use glitter glue to add buttons and trim.

11. Fit all the parts together and add any final embellishments of your own.

2 PETS

Getting Started With Cats

In this chapter we're going to make cats and dogs. Lots of them. But first, we need to think about what shapes we see when we look at a cat or dog. It helps to look at a sketch or picture of a real pet.

Of course you don't have to make your clay cat or dog look exactly like the real animal. You're an artist, so there are a lot of ways that you could choose to make your favorite pet. Whether it be exaggerating a few shapes or simplifying the whole animal by choosing to illustrate only its most basic features—the possibilities are endless.

So let's get started and see if we can make a really simple cat by using the most important shapes.

THREE VERY SIMPLE CATS

1 ROLL A BALL
Make one egg shape for the body and head. That's the main shape of most cats. Make small eggs for ears and a rope for the tail. Make tiny balls for the eyes and nose.

Body Shapes

Body — pink egg

Ears — 2 small pink eggs

Eyes — 2 tiny black balls

Nose — pink ball

Tail — pink rope

2 MAKE FACIAL FEATURES

Press the eyes into the front of the face. Use a cut straw tool to make the two curves for the mouth.

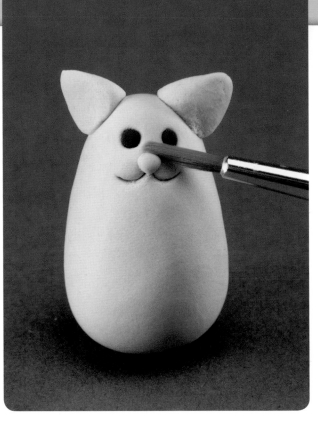

3 ADD THE NOSE, EARS AND TAIL

Position the nose. Use a brush to press down the top of the nose so it looks more like a triangle. Press the ears onto the head. Cats' ears don't stick straight up, out or down. They slant a bit to the side. Press the rope tail to the back of the body.

4 MAKE MORE CATS

Now create some more cats. Try starting with egg-shaped bodies that are not quite as round as the first cat's.

How Big Should the Pieces be?

You may wonder how big you should make each cat. Are the arms and legs too big? Too small? Just right? It doesn't matter so much how big each cat is as long as you have enough clay in the right colors to finish the project. What does matter is that each part is in proportion to the other parts. So, if you happen to make a big head, you probably should make a big body that matches it and do the same with the other body parts. Unless, of course, you choose to exaggerate and make an outrageous or unusual cat.

Whimsical Cats

HOW TO MAKE PLAYFUL CATS

We'll be using the same shapes as seen with the simple cats, but we'll be adding legs and a separate head when we make these two playful cats.

Body Shapes

Backbone — toothpick

Body — pink egg

Eyes — small black balls

Head — pink egg

Legs — 4 pink drumsticks

Nose — small pink ball

Tail — pink rope

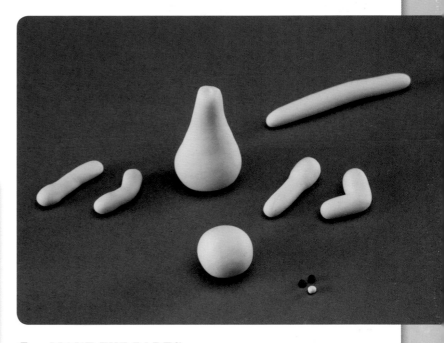

1 MAKE THE PARTS

First, shape the body so you'll know how big to make the other pieces. Do this by making an egg shape, then turn it into a short drumstick. Do the same with the arms and legs on a smaller scale. Then make a rope for the tail, a ball for the head and tiny balls for the nose and eyes.

BE CREATIVE!

Use your imagination to think of other ways to use what you've learned about working with clay.

GO ONLINE FOR MORE FUN!

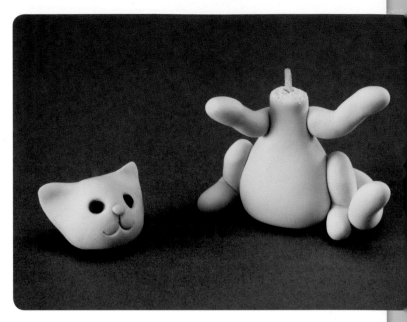

2 SHAPE THE HEAD

The head starts as a round ball. To make the ears, use your fingers to gently pull two softly rounded points from the clay. Pat each point smooth. To give shape to the ears, press and roll a round tool into the center of each ear.

3 PUT THE PIECES TOGETHER

Make the eyes, mouth and nose like you did for the simple cats. Then press the arms, legs and tail in place. Make sure to add a toothpick for the backbone and press the head onto the body. Then let dry.

4 FINISHING TOUCHES

Make the cat grin by pushing the blunt end of a knitting needle against the corners of its mouth. Then add a few cat toy accessories like a yarn ball made out of a long, skinny clay rope that is rolled up into a ball shape.

A Side View

If you look at a cat's head from the side, you'll see that it isn't really a ball shape. It's more like an egg shape that is tipped on its side.

1 SHAPE THE HEAD
To give more of a cat shape to this clay cat's head, roll the head ball into an egg shape. It will flatten a bit when you make the face.

2 MAKE FACIAL FEATURES
To make the mouth, use a cut-straw tool. Use a rounded tool to press in the eye sockets. Add the nose.

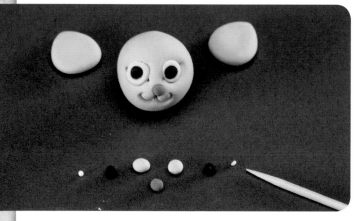

3 PERFECT THE EYES
This photo shows the size, the number and the color of pieces that are used for the eyes, ears and nose. Make the eyes by adding the biggest balls first. Press on the black pupil. Then, mark the corners of the eyes to make them a bit almond shaped.

4 ADD THE FINISHING TOUCHES
Press the head onto the body. Press the ears in place. Add the tiny white dots to the eyes. These are for the light reflection. If they're too big, they'll make the clay cat look blind.

Clothes for Cats

Just like some pet lovers dress up their real life animals, let's try dressing up our clay cats into some ballerina costumes. In this project you'll make a pink and purple outfit but the colors are really up to you, so have fun with it.

Body Shapes

Backbone — toothpick

Body — yellow egg

Head — completed head

Legs — 4 yellow drumsticks, 2 thicker for the back legs

Skirt — flattened rope of colored clay

Tail — yellow rope

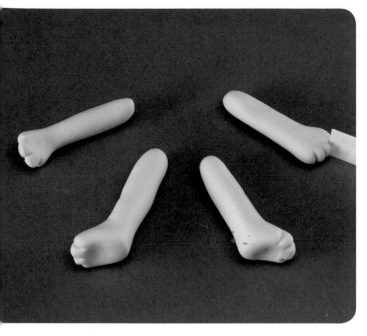

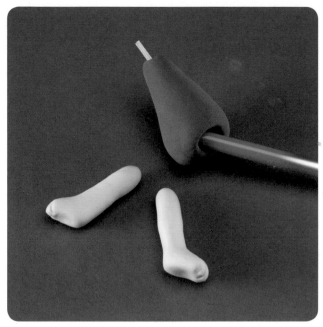

1 MAKE FINGERS, TOES AND HOLES

To add fingers and toes, use a plastic tool to cut in the lines. To make the holes in the leotard, use a rounded tool, such as a paintbrush handle. The holes need to be big enough for the legs to fit into them.

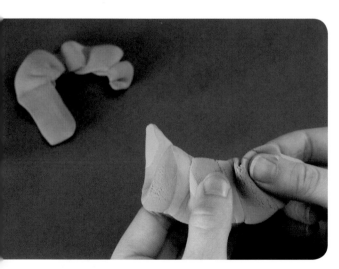

2 CHOOSE THE SKIRT

Here are two choices for the skirt. The striped one is made from a twisted pink and green rope that was flattened. To form the ruffles, make little folds along one side.

3 ADD IT ALL UP

Press the legs into the holes. Wrap the ruffle around the waist. Add the arms and head. You may have to prop the arms until they are thoroughly dry.

Realistic Cat Face

Look at the shapes on the cat's face. Do you see the eyelids and the three ball-like shapes that make up the chin and muzzle? There's also a long egg-shaped piece above the nose and between the eyes that needs to end somewhere. Now it's time to incorporate more cat-like features into our clay cats.

ADDING CAT FEATURES

Let's try using some new techniques to make this clay cat's face more realistic.

Body Shapes

Body — long oval

Ears — 2 flattened yellow eggs

Eyelids — 2 flattened yellow balls

Eyes — 2 tiny black balls and 2 slightly larger green balls

Head — yellow ball

Legs — 4 yellow ropes

Line between eyes — flattened, thin egg

Muzzle and chin — 3 yellow balls

Nose — black ball

Tail — long yellow rope

1 MAKE ROUND BALLS

To make the muzzle and chin, roll three small balls. Place one ball at the chin area. Press the other two balls just above that one. Use a round tool to make the eye sockets.

2 MAKE THE EYES AND EYELIDS

To make the eyes, press in green balls and then tiny black ones. Poke a hole in the center of each eye. Use a toothpick to mark the corners of the eyes. To make the eyelids, flatten two yellow balls. Cut the flattened balls in half. Place one half under each eye and one over each eye.

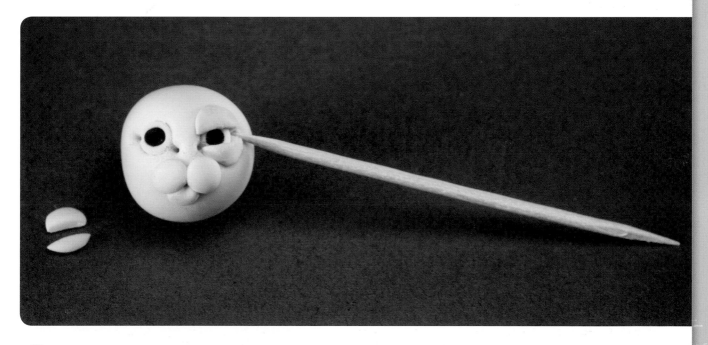

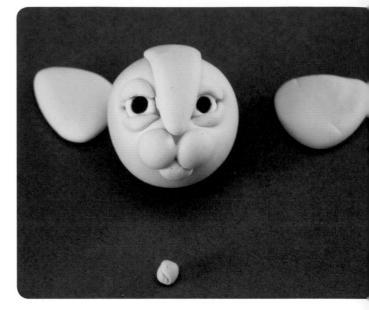

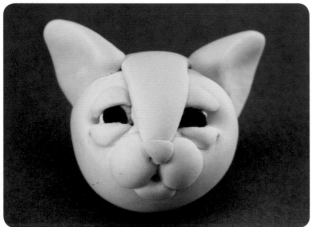

3 PUT THE HEAD TOGETHER

To make the section above the nose, roll a long egg shape that is narrow enough to fit between the eyes. Flatten the long egg shape. Press it over the muzzle and up over the top of the head. Add the flattened egg-shaped ears. Roll a small ball for the nose. Position the nose. Use a brush to shape it into a triangle. Use a toothpick to make nostrils and to open the mouth.

LIE DOWN

To make the cat lying down, roll a large oval shape for the body. Add the front legs, a short piece of toothpick for attaching the head, the tail and the head.

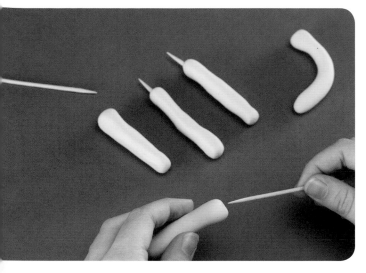
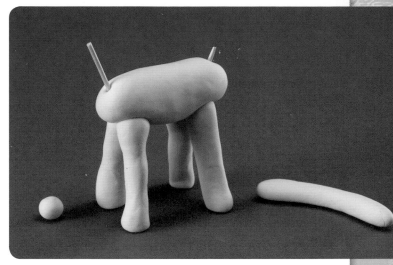

4 MAKE THE LEGS

To make legs for a standing cat, make four ropes for the legs. Press a toothpick into the center of each. Roll a rope for the tail.

Press the legs into the body. Add a short piece of toothpick to hold the head and another to hold the tail. Make a ball for the neck.

5 FINISHING TOUCHES

Add the rest of the pieces. Prop the body up until the clay dries.

What Makes a Dog Look Like a Dog

GIVE DOGS SOMETHING TO BARK ABOUT

There are so many shapes for dogs. Some have long noses. Others have short ones. Some have ears that stand straight up. Others have ears that droop down, almost to the ground. Some have long tails, and some have none at all. So what is that one indistinguishable feature that makes a dog look like a dog?

It can vary. But follow along as I transform a pile of clay into man's best friend, using basic dog-like features.

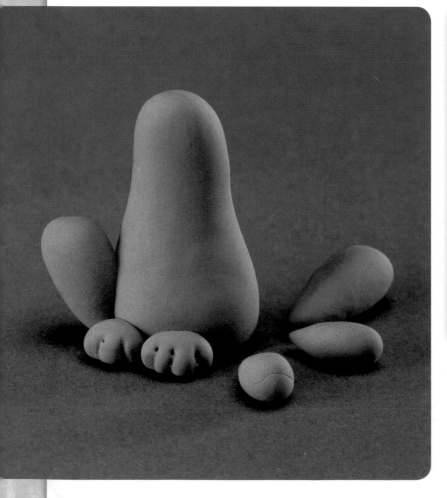

Body Shapes

Body — fat brown drumstick

Ears — 2 flattened brown eggs

Eyes — 2 tiny black balls

Feet — 4 brown small eggs

Legs — 2 medium sized brown eggs

Nose — black ball

Tail — short brown rope

1 MAKE THE BODY PARTS
Make a fat drumstick shape that looks almost like an egg. For the feet, make four small eggs and two medium-sized eggs for the back legs. Then use a tool to press lines in for the toes.

2 FORM THE MOUTH AND EYES
Use a straw tool and a toothpick to make the mouth. Make holes for the eyes and drop in black eyeballs.

3 MAKE THE TAIL
Flatten the eggs for the ears and press in place. Let the tops droop. Add a short rope for a tail.

4 ADD THE NOSE
Add a black ball for the nose.

Make a Variety of Dogs

CHANGE THE SHAPES, CHANGE THE SIZE

Try rearranging or exaggerating some of your dog's clay features to discover new ways of making your pet look different from other dogs, using the same basic shapes.

Body Shapes

Body — yellow egg

Ears — 2 flattened yellow eggs

Eyebrows — 2 tiny black ropes

Eyes — 2 tiny black balls, 2 slightly bigger brown balls and 2 slightly bigger white balls

Head — yellow egg

Legs — 4 yellow drumsticks (make the front legs smaller)

Neck bone — toothpick

Nose — tiny black ball

Tail — yellow rope

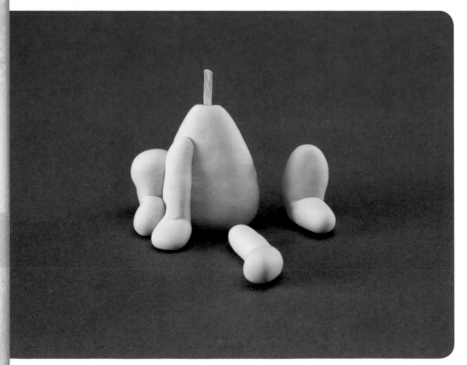

1 MAKE THE BODY
Start with an egg shape for the body and add the toothpick for the neck bone.

Make the front legs and back legs from drumstick shapes. Notice that the back legs are fatter and shorter than the front ones. Press the legs to the body.

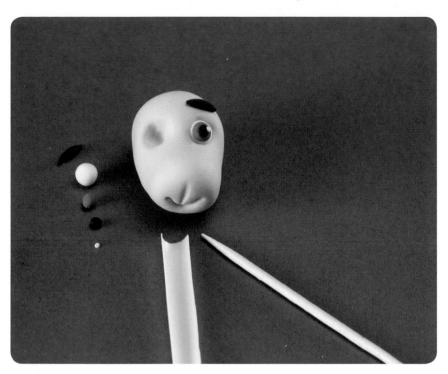

2 MAKE THE HEAD

The head is an egg shape. Add the features using a straw tool and toothpick. Make holes for the eyes. Push in the bigger white balls. Add the other balls in layers, with the tiny white one last. Press on tiny ropes for the eyebrows. Add a round black ball for the nose.

3 ADD THE EARS AND TAIL

Press the head onto the body. Add flattened egg-shaped ears and a rope tail. Make marks to separate the toes.
Now try making other variations of clay dogs with unusual features.

Mix It Up

When making a specific kind of dog, it's helpful to look at a picture of that dog. That's what I did when I decided to make a Pug. I used a picture to help me decide the shape, size and color of each of the pieces. I chose to add just the most important details, like the black ears and muzzle, flat nose, short legs and thick body.

Body Shapes

Body — marbled brown and white egg

Ears — 2 black teardrops

Eyebrows/eyelids — 2 tiny brown flattened ropes, 2 brown teardrops

Eyes — 2 tiny white balls, 2 slightly bigger black balls and 2 bigger light brown balls

Head — brown ball

Leg bones — 4 toothpicks

Legs — 4 brown drumsticks

Muzzle and chin — 2 black eggs and a black ball

Neck bone — toothpick

Nose — black ball

Tail — marbled brown and white rope

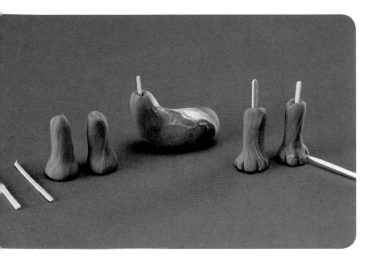

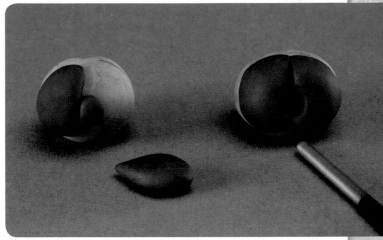

1 MAKE THE BODY AND LEGS

Make an egg-shaped body. Turn up the small end. Press in a piece of toothpick for the neck bone. Make very short drumsticks for legs. Add toothpick bones. Cut in lines between the toes. Press the legs into the body.

2 MAKE THE MUZZLE

Because Pugs have a very short muzzle, make the head as a ball shape. For the muzzle, roll two black egg shapes and one small black ball. Press the ball on first, for the chin. Then press an egg onto each side, over the top of the chin. Use a paintbrush handle to push in a hole for the mouth.

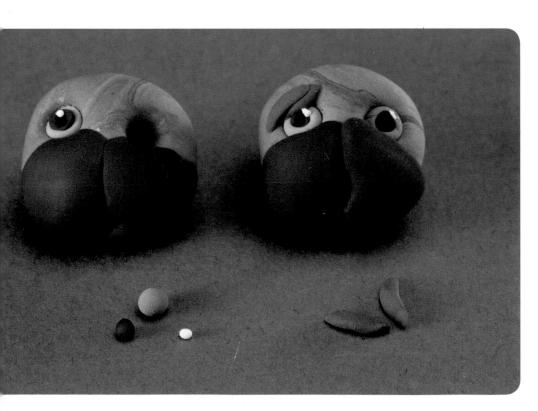

3 ADD THE EYES

Make a hole for each eye. Roll a brown ball, a black one and a tiny white one for each eye. Press in place, starting with the brown ball. For the eyelids and eyebrows, roll dark brown, skinny teardrop shapes. Flatten them. Press these in layers over the eyes.

Finish the clay Pug by adding short, teardrop-shaped ears, a rope tail and, last of all, the nose. Make sure to poke holes in the nose.

Make an Appointment at the Dog Salon

In order to make curly or shaggy hair for your clay dogs, the secret is to make a hairless dog first—without ears, nose or eyes. Let this dry overnight or longer. Then, when it's hard, you can add more layers and the final details.

Body Shapes

Body —brown egg

Ears — 2 flattened brown eggs

Eyes — 2 tiny black balls

Head — brown egg

Legs — 4 brown drumsticks

Neck bone/backbone — toothpicks

Nose — tiny black ball

Tail — brown rope

DRY TIME

The standing clay dogs have toothpicks in their legs to help make them strong. They all have toothpick backbones. Leave one or two dog's mouths wide open so there will be room to add tongues later.

GETTING A MOP CUT

To make the hair, roll ropes of clay. Flatten the ropes and rip them into pieces. Press the ripped pieces to the body, starting at the feet. Keep adding layers until the whole body is covered. Press in eyes and add a nose, ears and a tail. Add a few extra pieces around the eyes so it looks like they're peeking out at you.

DRAW HAIR WITH A TOOTH-PICK

To make sculpted hair, press flat pieces of brown clay over the hardened body. Work in sections so the pieces don't dry out too fast. Use a toothpick or a plastic tool to draw in the hair lines. For the tongue, roll a pink egg shape. Flatten it. Use a toothpick to press it into the mouth. Add the eyes, ears, nose and tail.

MAKE A HAPPY SMILE

Pull some of the clay down around the mouth. Use a knitting needle and a tooth-pick to press in the corners of the mouth and give the dog a happy grin. Because the mouth was open when it hardened, there is room to push the clay deeper into the mouth to make a wider grin.

MAKE BANGS

Roll little ropes of clay. Flatten them and press over the top of the head.

Get Out the Dishes

Have you ever thought about being a dish designer? This is your chance. Choose any color of clay, but white clay is fun and easy to decorate with markers.

1 HOW TO MAKE PLATES

To make plates, start with a ball of clay. The size depends on the type of plate that you want to make. Make big ones for platters and small ones for salad plates. Flatten the ball, then press the middle with something flat to indent it. Here I'm using the end of the glitter glue bottle. Let it dry.

2 HOW TO MAKE CUPS

Roll a ball, then roll it into a short rope. Use a paintbrush handle to press into the center and hollow it out. While the cup is still on the handle, roll the cup against the table to smooth the edges. Remove and let dry.

3 HOW TO MAKE BOWLS

Roll a ball, then hollow out the center with a paintbrush handle or other rounded tool. Use your finger to press down on the edges to round and smooth them and to flatten the bottom. Let dry.

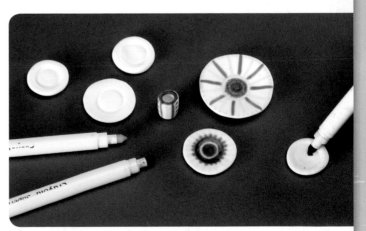

4 ADD DESIGNS

Once the dishes are dry, use markers to add color and patterns.

Salad and Sandwiches

These tables are made from blocks that are covered with paper. You could also use small cardboard boxes, recycled containers or folded cardstock.

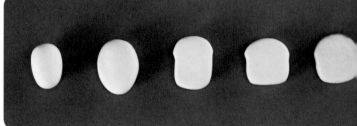

STIR UP SOME DIP

Mix up several colors of clay that remind you of your favorite dips. Here I'm using white for a ranch dip and a light brown for hummus. You'll also need a clay bowl that is dry and hard.

GIVE IT TEXTURE

Press the clay into the bowl, then use a toothpick and an old toothbrush to give texture to the top. Make it look like it's been stirred or is kind of lumpy. After you have filled the bowl, decorate the outside with markers.

BAKE SOME BREAD

For each slice of bread that you'll be making, roll an egg shape. Do you want them all the same size, or do you want some to look like different kinds of bread? It's your choice. Flatten the egg. Press against the sides with a flat tool to make them look indented. Press the bottom edge to flatten it. Let it dry, then paint the edges with brown watercolor paint. Use a damp cloth to wipe off extra paint.

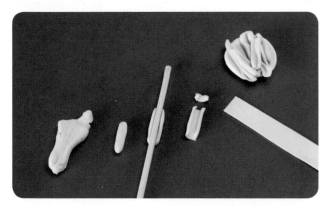

CHOP UP SOME CELERY

To make a plate of celery, use mostly white clay mixed with a tiny bit of green and yellow. If it's too bright, add a tiny bit of brown. Roll short ropes, then press the ropes against the toothpick or skewer to hollow out one side. Trim the ends. Stack on a plate. You could also let them dry, then fill them with brown clay for peanut butter or white for cream cheese.

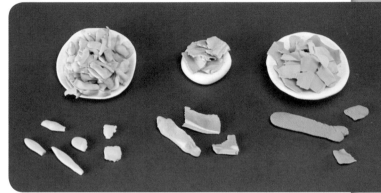

CLEAN SOME VEGETABLES

Tomatoes: Roll tiny balls of red clay.

Carrots: Roll orange balls, then turn them into teardrop shapes by rolling on one side of the ball.

Cauliflower and broccoli: Roll egg shapes, then use a toothpick to give them texture and a lumpy shape.

GRATE, SLICE AND SHRED THE SANDWICH FIXINGS

For cheese, roll tiny yellow ropes, then chop up into smaller pieces. For shaved ham, turkey or roast beef, mix a color of clay that looks like the food. For ham or turkey, start with white clay and add a little pink and brown to it. Leave the colors a bit streaky. For roast beef, start with brown clay. Roll clay ropes, then flatten them very thin. Pull and rip the edges.

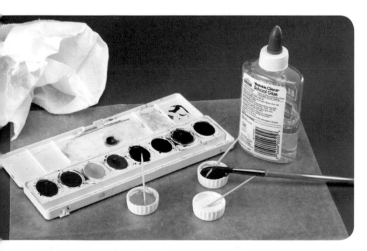

OPEN UP THE KETCHUP, MUSTARD AND DRESSING

Clear glue is the main ingredient in these recipes. Put a small amount of glue into a recycled bottle cap or other tiny container. Using a wet brush, pick up some water-color paint, then drip it over the glue in the cap. Use a toothpick to mix it up.

MAKE A SANDWICH AND BUILD A SALAD

Make the sandwich just like you would make a real sandwich, choosing your favorite fixings. Drip the glue ketchup, mustard or dressing over the top. Add the other half of the sandwich. Let dry, then cut it into two pieces.

Then take a trip to the salad bar. Pick what you like, then pour some glue "dressing" over the top. The glue will help hold all the little pieces together. If you want a white salad dressing, use a glue that dries white.

Desserts

You can never go wrong with cookies and doughnuts!

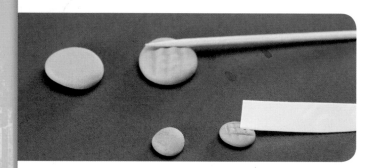

PEANUT BUTTER COOKIES

To make peanut butter cookies, mix a tiny bit of brown clay into white. Roll balls, then flatten them with your finger. Use a toothpick or a plastic tool to press crisscross lines into the tops.

BAKED COOKIES

To "bake" the cookies, let them dry, then brush the tops with brown watercolor paint. Wipe off any extra paint.

CHOCOLATE CRINKLES

To make chocolate crinkles, roll balls of brown clay. You choose the size. Add crinkles to the top by pressing with an old toothbrush. Let dry.

PEANUT BUTTER BLOSSOMS

The trick to making peanut butter blossoms is to make the chocolate candy kisses first. Roll brown teardrops with flattened bottoms, then let them dry while you're mixing up the cookie dough color. Roll a ball of "dough." Flatten a bit. Press a small hole in the top. Add the clay candy kiss while the cookie is still soft. Let dry, then "bake" by brushing with brown watercolor paint.

SANDWICH COOKIES

To make these layered cookies, roll two dark brown balls and one white one. Flatten all three balls just a little bit. Stack the layers. Press the top with something that has a design in it. Let dry.

This close-up shows how the design in the glitter glue cap was perfect for making a design in the cookie.

Baker's Recipe: Glazed Doughnuts!

Chocolate donut glaze
Dark brown clay
Glue that dries clear
Light brown clay (Mix together orange, brown and white clay)

Roll balls of each color. Then leave the light brown balls alone since they're going to be our doughnuts. Flatten the dark brown balls, which will serve as the chocolate frosting on our doughnuts. Place the chocolate frosting layer over the doughnut layer. Use a tool, such as a paintbrush handle, to make a hole in the center. Drip clear glue over the top to make the frosting shiny.

BANANA SPLITS

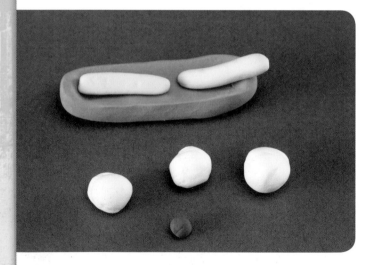

1 MAKE THE DISH AND ICE CREAM

Make a clay dish from a long clay oval. Hollow out the inside by pressing it with a rounded tool like a fat paint brush handle.

Then make some bananas (a long skinny clay oval sliced in half), balls of ice cream (white clay balls that are textured by rolling against a toothbrush) and cherries (red balls of clay).

2 ADD CHOCOLATE SAUCE

Make "chocolate sauce" from clear glue that was colored with brown watercolor paint. Assemble the banana split, then drizzle sauce over the top. Let dry.

CUPCAKES

These cupcakes are made up of three layers of clay. They represent the cupcake paper, the cake itself and the frosting. Mix up a color of clay for each part. What flavor of cupcake and frosting would you like to make? Choose colors of clay that make you think of those flavors.

How to Make a Cupcake:

1. The Cupcake Paper: Roll a ball. Flatten it slightly. Use a tool to add ridge marks all along the sides.
2. The Cupcake: Roll a ball. Flatten it so it looks like the top of a cupcake. Layer it on top of the cupcake paper.
3. The Frosting: Roll a ball. Flatten it. Place it over the cupcake.
4. The Decorations: Add a rolled-up rose or tiny balls and flattened teardrops to represent flowers and leaves. Drip clear glitter glue over the top.

Add variety to your clay cupcakes. Sprinkle bits of colored clay on top for chocolate sprinkles or candy bits. Make cherries. Make some super sized. Use different colors of glitter glue.

BIG CUPCAKES

The cupcake paper is a plastic bottle cap. Stuff the bottle cap with a piece of paper toweling. Add the cupcake piece, the frosting and the decorations over the top.

These larger cupcakes are made just like the little ones, except for the cupcake paper.

Beauty Salon

Before we get into creating some different hairstyles and accessories, here are a few simple steps you can follow to create an actual salon for your world in clay. You'll use many of the techniques you've already mastered.

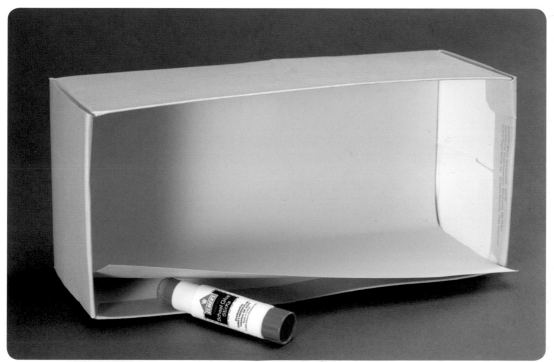

1 DESIGN A SHOP

Turn a shoebox into a room by first covering the inside with colored paper. Add windows, doors, signs, switchplates and rugs. Then look at it again and see what else it might need.

2 NAME THAT PLACE

Use the box lid as a roof. Make a name sign to fit the front edge. Glue it in place.

3 HANG THINGS ON THE WALLS

Make extra hats, scarves and purses to hang on the walls of the salon. Pushpins work as hooks, but be careful because they'll go through the shoebox and may be sharp on the other side.

4 COVER THE BACK

This is the back side of the shoebox. Cover up the sharp pins and keep your fingers safe by pressing a piece of air dry clay over all of the pins, then let them dry.

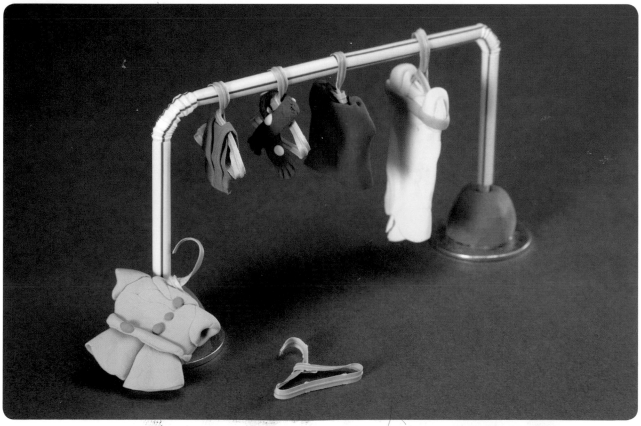

5 MAKE CLOTHES AND TINY HANGERS

Create little hangers from a folded twist tie, the kind that come with plastic bags or garbage bags. Then make clothes to fit onto the hangers. Design them like you would dresses for paper dolls, but you'll need a front and a back so you can sandwich the hanger in the middle. Add buttons and fun details.

6 MAKE A CLOTHING RACK

The clothing rack is made from two flexible drinking straws. A piece of bamboo skewer is put into each piece to keep them straight. They're supported in a stand that's made from air dry clay. Heavy washers are glued to the bottom of each stand to keep them from tipping over.

7 MAKE PROPS AND ACCESSORIES

The furniture in the salon is mostly made from blocks. The mirrors can be found in the mosaic department at a craft store. The brooms are pieces of bamboo skewer stuck into layers of clay fringe, made the same way that you make hair.

8 ODDS AND ENDS

The bottles, hair dryer, scissors and combs are all made from air dry clay.

9 MIRROR

The mirror has a piece of bamboo skewer inside to support it. The yellow and orange parts are air dry clay. Glitter glue was used for the designs.

Style Tips for Clay Hair

The great thing about clay hair is that you don't have to wait for it to grow out. Just change it to any style that fits your interest!

1 THE FRINGE CUT
Create a shaggy fringe cut by starting with a flattened ball of clay. Press four lines across the clay, like you would when cutting a pie, but be careful not to press all the way through the clay. Now make little lines in each section.

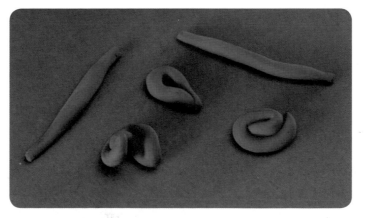

2 ARRANGE THE FRINGE
Lay the fringed circle on top of the head. Arrange the edges with a paintbrush or toothpick.

3 AN ELEGANT UPDO
Change the plain, shaggy cut into an elegant one by adding little clay curls and twists on top. Just poke them in place and style.

Tips for Styling With String or Yarn

This looks a little weird but, if you're going to use string for hair, you'll need a place to stick it. So go ahead and poke those holes. If you don't like the style, you can always cover up the holes with clay hair. Let the head and hair dry thoroughly before adding the string hair.

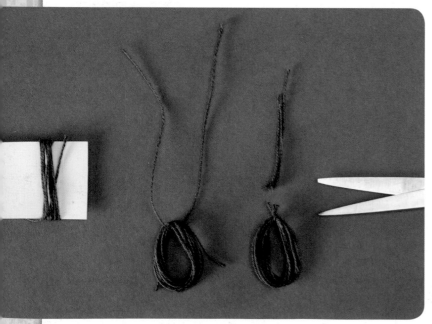

1 PICK YOUR COLORS

Choose a color of string or yarn. How long would you like the hair to be? Cut a piece of cardboard that is that wide. Wrap the string around it. Trim off the extra string.

2 LOOP THE HOLES

Use a toothpick to stick the string loops into the holes. Once you've decided exactly how you want them, glue them in place.

3 STYLE IT

Leave the loops the way they are, or trim off the ends.

4 CHANGE IT UP

Try a variety of hairstyles, mix and match to make the haircut that fits your clay doll best.

Make a Wreath

Materials

12" (30cm) chenille stems: 4 light green, 3 dark green

Air dry clay: colors to make pale pink and spring green

Ribbon: 3 yards (3m) of 1" (3cm) wide pale green, 1 yard (3m) of 1" (3cm) wide pale pink, 2 yards (2m) of ½" (2cm) wide pale yellow

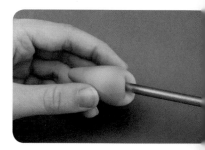

1 CUT THE STEMS
Cut the yellow ribbon into one 1 yard (1m) piece and six 6" (15cm) pieces, and cut the dark green chenille stems in half. Discard one. Turn all ends into a tight loop. When you're done, you'll have four long ones and five short ones.

2 MAKE THE LEAVES
Roll five green balls, each about the size of a big grape. Roll into teardrop shapes. Make a hole in the large end of each teardrop.

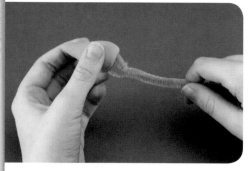

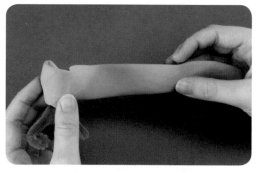

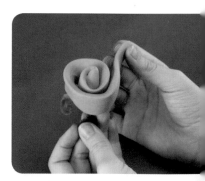

3 CURL LEAVES AROUND THE STEMS
Poke a curled end of the long chenille stem into the hole. Then pinch the clay around the curled stem so the loop is trapped inside. Repeat this by making leaves on each end of the four long stems. You'll end up with eight leaves.

4 MAKE THE ROSES
Twist the center of the five short stems into a small loop. The wreath will look more graceful if the roses are different sizes. Start the first one by making a 6"(15cm) long clay rope that is about as fat as a grape. The next ones can be bigger or smaller. Flatten the rope. Twist one end of the strip of clay tightly around one of the center loops.

5 WRAP LOOSELY
Continue wrapping the strip of clay. Keep it a bit loose. Be careful that it doesn't get tall or it will look like a pinecone.

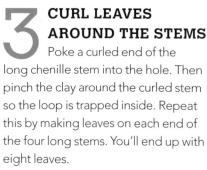

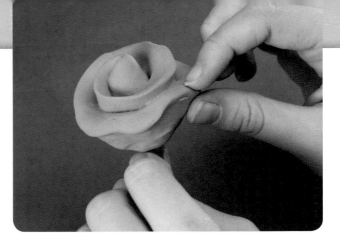

6 FLIP OVER
Turn the rose upside down and pinch the bottom.

7 TRAP THE LOOP AND ROLL THE EDGES
Trap the loop inside so the rose will stay in place. Roll over the edges of the rose. Repeat steps 4-7 with the other four center loops.

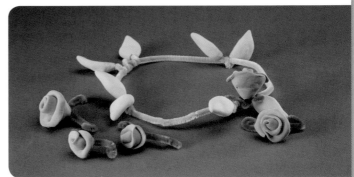

8 LET DRY
Let all the pieces dry overnight, or longer, until they are thoroughly dry and hard.

9 MAKE A CIRCLE
Carefully wrap the ends of the long stems together to make a circle. Be gentle. The leaves and roses are quite strong, but they will break. Decide where you want the roses to be. To hold them in place, twist their stems around the larger circle.

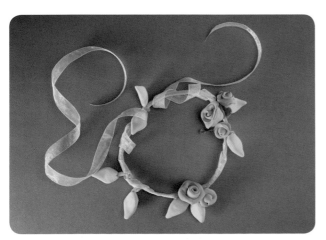

10 WRAP WITH RIBBON
Decide how long you'd like the ribbon tails to be. Starting at the back of the wreath and leaving the tail hanging, wrap the 3-yard (3m) piece of green ribbon around the wreath. Wrap all the way around, ending with the second tail. Knot the two ribbons together in the back.

11 FINISH UP
Tie the 1 yard (1m) pieces of pink and yellow ribbon in place. Tie the short pieces of yellow ribbon around the wreath. Use them to cover up places where the wires were twisted together.

Visit www.impact-books.com/clay-creation-workshop-bonus-material for more projects! **61**

MAKE A ROSE AND RIBBON CLIP!

Do you love the roses, but don't feel like making such a big project? Well, good news! Here's a mini version of the rose wreath, with just one flower, two leaves and a few pieces of ribbon.

Create a rose, as shown in the previous project. Let the flower dry thoroughly, then wrap the chenille stem around the barrette. Tie on the ribbons.

Materials

3 pieces of ribbon — colors of your choice, each about 12" (30cm) long

6" (15cm) piece of green chenille stem with a rose on one end and a leaf on the other. (Make both using the instructions for the leaf and rose in the wreath project, but put both on the same stem.)

Barrette clip

MAKE A WREATH FOR YOUR CLAY CHARACTERS TO WEAR!

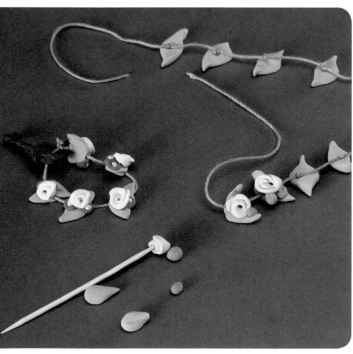

First, cut a piece of string or yarn that is at least 4" (10cm) longer than what you'll need to go around one of the clay doll's heads. Then tie knots in the string wherever you would like a leaf or flower to be.

Start making a flower and two leaves. While they are still soft, sandwich two leaves under the knot with the flower on top. Repeat with the rest of the knots. Make the wreath more interesting by adding tiny, colorful balls. Let dry thoroughly. Then tie the two ends of the string together.

5 BEADS, BAUBLES AND BLING

How to Make Tiny Necklaces for Your Characters

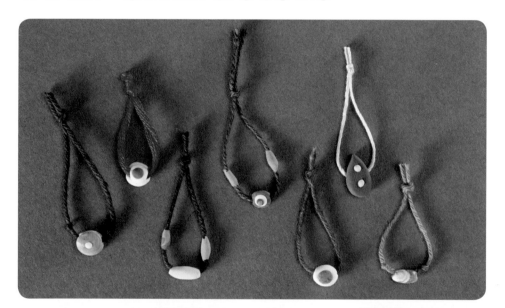

CHOOSE THREAD

Choose colorful string or embroidery thread. Make extras so your characters can change the jewelry with their outfits.

TIE KNOTS FOR BEADS

For one bead, tie a knot where you want the bead to be. Make a bead. Put a hole in it. Poke the knot into the hole. Pinch the clay around the knot. Let it dry. Tie the necklace ends in a knot. Trim the ends of the string.

ADD CLAY BEADS

For this necklace, make two knots in the string. Leave room in the middle for the clay bead. Wrap a piece of clay around the string. Roll the bead to smooth the seam. Let dry, then tie the knot and cut the string ends.

How to Make Bigger Beads

IDEAS FOR DIFFERENT BEADS TO MAKE

Look at the beads on the next three pages. Choose whatever colors or shapes you like best, then make a pile of them. When you start to string them, you'll probably wish that you had a few more. So create some extra ones in different color combinations. Make some big, some small.

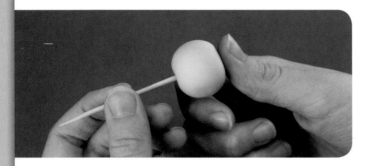

1 MAKE A HOLE
To make a clean hole in the bead, press a toothpick through the center just far enough to prick through on the other side. You'll feel it with your finger. Go slow, the point is sharp.

2 MAKE THE SIDES EVEN
Now take the bead off the toothpick and turn it around. Make the hole going in from the other side. This will even up the hole so both sides look the same.

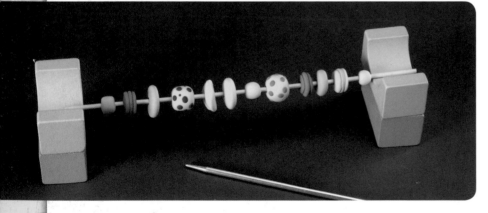

TIPS

1. Make the pieces quite thick. Thin pieces will break easily.

2. Be sure the beads are very dry and hard before you string them.

3. Keep your beads away from water. Water makes the clay sticky.

3 WIDEN THE HOLE
Be sure that the hole is big enough for whatever cord or string you'll be using. One way to make bigger holes is to use bigger tools. My favorites are toothpicks, knitting needles and bamboo skewers.
While these beads are drying on the skewer, to keep them from sticking, twist them around a few times while they're still soft.

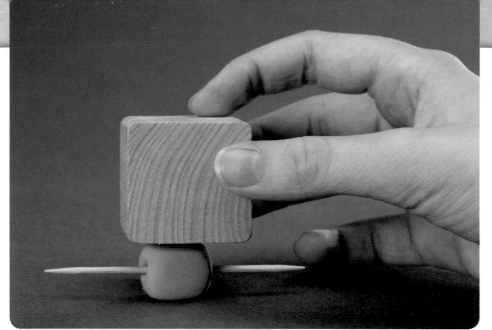

Square Beads
To make square beads, start with a ball. Press a toothpick or skewer through the center. Press a flat object on one side of the bead. Turn the bead. Repeat. Twist the toothpick to be sure the bead hasn't stuck, then let dry.

Striped Marble Beads
Striped beads are made from a rope of marbled colors. Twist the ends of the ropes in opposite directions until the stripes start going around and around the bead. Cut the rope into chunks. Put a hole first through one end of the bead and then the other.

Swirled Marble Beads
Marbled or swirled beads are made by mixing two or more colors together. Stop mixing before the colors get too muddy. Break off pieces of clay and roll beads.

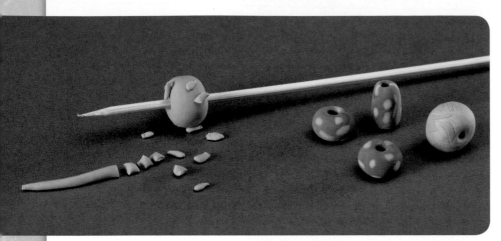

Confetti Beads

Confetti beads are my favorite because they're easy and colorful. Choose two or more colors of clay. Roll a bead from one color. Make a rope from the other color. Chop the rope up into tiny pieces. They don't all have to be the same size or shape. Put the bead on a skewer. Roll the soft bead across the chopped up pieces so that the bead picks them up. Roll the bead in your hand to smooth the surface. Remake the hole. Let dry.

Polka Dot Beads

These beads are almost like the confetti beads, but the tiny pieces are each rolled into balls before they are added to the bigger bead. These take more time but can be worth it.

Sandwich Beads

These beads are layers of color that are stacked together. To begin, make different sizes of balls. Flatten balls. Stack the resulting circles in three or four layers. Make a hole in the center, then let it dry.

Striped Beads

Make more distinct stripes by laying ropes of two different colors next to each other. Twist the ropes together until stripes form. Roll the doubled rope to smooth the sides. Cut chunks and make beads.

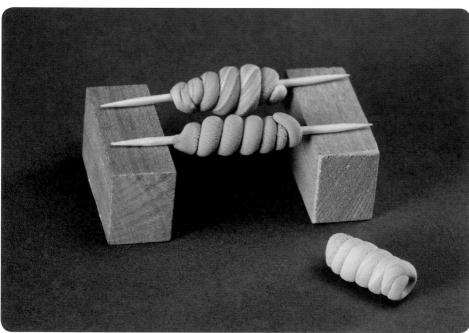

Rope Beads

Roll long, skinny ropes of clay. Wrap clay ropes around a toothpick or skewer. Make them short, long, fat or skinny. Twist to make sure they aren't stuck, then let dry.

Wavy Disk Beads

Roll and flatten different sized balls of clay. For added texture, press with a toothbrush. Twist the edges. Let dry.

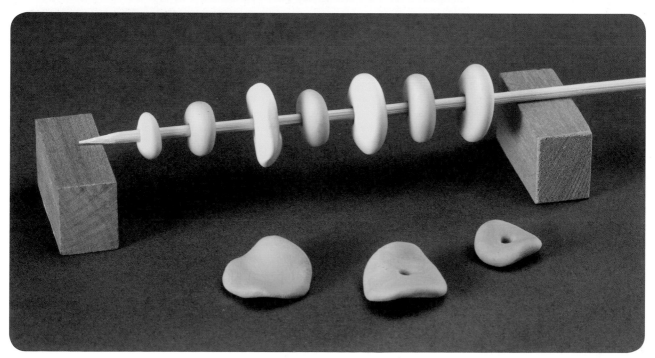

Make Something to Wear

STRING A BRACELET

String beads onto a cord, then tie the ends together. Use one string or two. Or you might choose to use elastic or stretchy cord that is available at craft stores. Check in the jewelry department at your local craft store to see what types of cording it carries. Just be sure that the holes in your beads are big enough for the cord to fit through.

DESIGN A NECKLACE

Ribbon makes a beautiful neck-lace, but sometimes it's hard to get it through the hole in the bead. One solution is to fold the ribbon over a piece of wire or string. Then put the smaller wire or string through the hole first. Now pull the ribbon through.

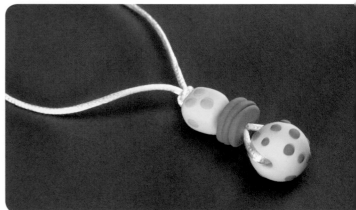

DIFFERENT BEADS

You can string lots of different kinds of beads on one rib-bon, or try making beads that are just a few colors and all the same shape.

STRING THE BEADS AND TIE THE KNOT

Start this necklace by putting the string through one bead. Then put the strings together and put both ends through a second and third bead. Both of those beads will need to have big holes. Tie a knot on top after the third bead.

CREATE A CLIP DANGLE

Some of your little beads will be perfect to use in this yarn and bead clip dangle. Make it long or short. Add just a few beads or a whole bunch. Change the color. Make it yours.

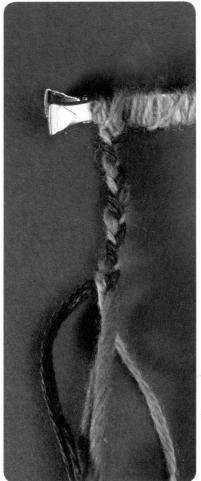

Materials

Barrette

Beads

Yarn — three colors, 1 yard (1m) of each

1 FOLD THE YARN

Fold the yarn in half. Tie the center of each piece of yarn around the barrette so the tails are the same length. You'll have six tails hanging down when you're done.

2 ARRANGE THE TAILS

Bring all six tails to one spot on the barrette. Divide the tails into three groups of two, then begin to braid.

3 BRAID

Keep braiding until the braid is as long as you'd like it to be, or until you have only 3" (8cm) of string left. Tie the ends together so the braid doesn't unravel. Add beads. Tie knots at the end of each strand so the beads won't fall off. You may have to make double knots or even triple knots.

6 RECREATION

How to Make Equipment for the Gym

You can use air dry clay to create miniature versions of a lot of the things that you might find in a gym. Here are a few ideas to get you started.

INDOORS

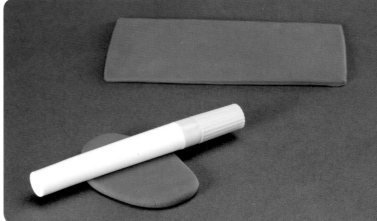

PICK A WORKOUT

The mats and barbells are all made from air dry clay. The barbell is made from a toothpick and it's painted green to match the mat.

ROLL SOME EXERCISE MATS

To make the mats, roll a fat rope that's as long as you want the mat to be. Flatten the rope with your hand. To make it very smooth, roll across the top with a smooth, round tool. Here I'm using a marker. Trim the edges so they're square.

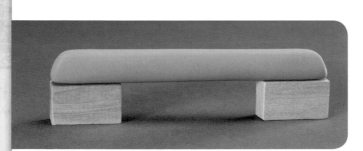

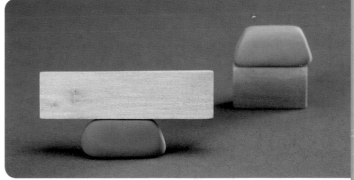

MAKE A BALANCE BEAM

To make the balance beam, find two blocks to use as supports. If you don't have any blocks, then try making your own out of clay.

To make the top piece, roll a clay rope that is wide enough for one of the girls to stand on. Use your fingers and then a smooth rod to roll and shape the beam. Let it dry flat, then put it on the supports after it's dry.

MAKE A VAULT

Roll a short rope from clay. The rope needs to be fat enough for one of the girls to stand on. Flatten the rope slightly with a smooth, flat tool. Press the ends at a slant. Place the vault on top of a block for support.

Clothes for Movement

HOW TO MAKE A DANCE OR GYMNASTICS COSTUME

1 PICK COLORS AND SHAPES

To make a dance costume, choose a color, then make an egg that's the size of the doll's body. Flatten a piece of skin-colored clay to wrap around the top of the egg. Add a toothpick and a wrapped rope for the neck. Press into the two flat spots where the legs will fit.

2 MAKE LEGS AND SLIPPERS

Make the legs and feet as one piece. Make a rope for the leg, then bend the rope at the heel to shape the foot. How long do you want the foot to be? Cut off extra clay from the top of the leg. Let the legs dry a bit before adding the ballet slippers.

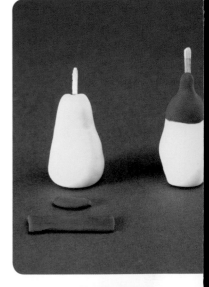

To make the ballet slippers, flatten and cut a piece of clay that is twice as long as the foot and just a little bit wider. Wrap this around the foot. Overlap the seam in the back. Fold the extra clay to the bottom of the foot and smooth the edges.

To make the straps, roll a skinny rope. Lay the middle of the rope over the top of the foot. Wrap one end of the rope to the back of the foot, then bring it around to the front of the shoe on the opposite side. Cut off any extra clay, then repeat with the other end.

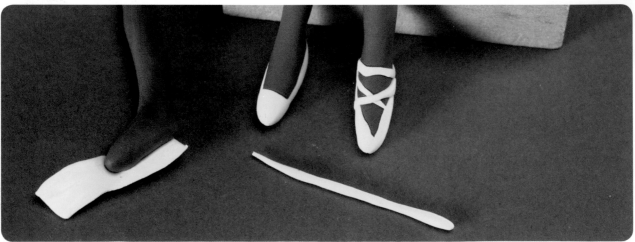

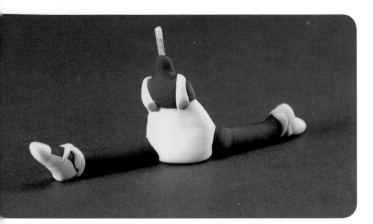

3 ADD STRAPS AND BUTTONS

Press the legs to the body. Add flat, skinny ropes for straps and tiny balls for buttons. You could stop here, or you could go to the next step and make a skirt. If you're going to add a skirt, let the body dry in this position first so the legs will stay straight. You may have to prop it up.

4 MAKE A RUFFLED SKIRT

To make the ruffle, first decide how wide you want the skirt to be. If the skirt is 2" (5cm) wide or long, roll a rope that is half that width, or 1" (3cm) wide. Flatten the rope so you have a long strip. Pick it up and fold along the top edge so you have lots of little overlapping gathers. Leave the other edge straight.

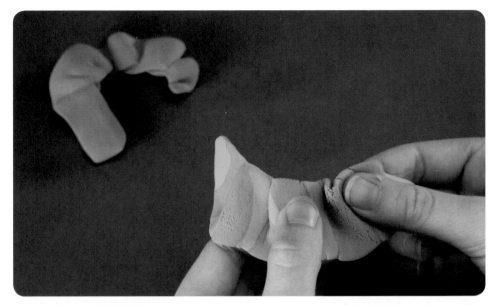

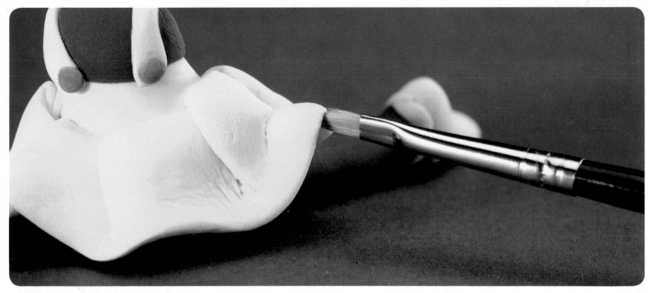

5 WRAP THE SKIRT AROUND

Wrap the ruffle around the waist. If it doesn't go all the way around, make another piece of ruffle and tuck it in. Use a brush to adjust the ruffle edges. Add the arms and head. Prop everything until it is thoroughly dry.

Everyday Workout Clothes

HOW TO MAKE SHORTS

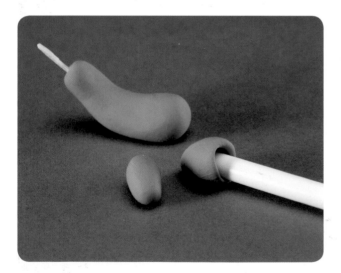

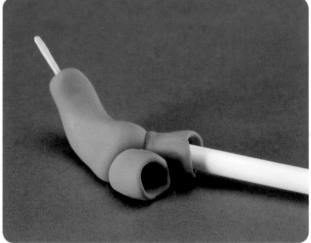

1 CHOOSE A CLAY COLOR
Choose a color of clay, then roll an egg for the body. Stretch the egg a bit, then lay it down. Tip up the small end. Add a toothpick. Make two ovals for the pant legs and hollow out the middle with a rounded tool.

2 PRESS THE PANT LEGS
While each pant leg is still on the tool, press it onto the body.

HOW TO MAKE SHOES

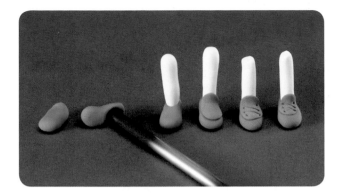 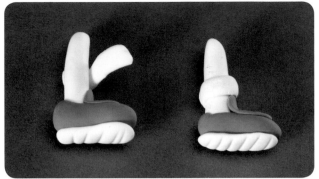

1 MAKE SHOE AND LEG SHAPES

Make two egg shapes for the shoes. Use a rounded paintbrush handle to hollow out their middles. Make ropes for legs and put a rope into each shoe. Press a flattened oval to the front of each shoe. Use a toothpick to poke holes for the shoestrings, and use a knife or plastic tool to mark in shoestring lines.

2 MAKE THE SOLES

To make soles for the shoes, press a flattened egg to the bottom of each shoe. Use a tool to mark in the tread lines. For the sock cuffs, wrap a strip of clay around the leg. Press the shoe legs into the pant legs.

HOW TO MAKE A TANK TOP

1 FLATTEN AND ARRANGE CLAY

Flatten two strips of skin-colored clay, one to wrap around the top of the body and a smaller strip for the neck. Put these in place. Make the arms and hands. Press these to the body. Flatten short strips of colored clay, two for the straps and one to fit across the front of the tank top. If you'd like, add further embellishments to the tank top, such as a varsity letter. Prop so the body dries in this position, and don't forget to add the head!

Make A Basketball Or Volleyball Net

Use flexible straws as supports for both the volleyball net and the basketball hoop. Pieces of bamboo skewers are put inside of the straws to hold them up straight. The bottom stand is air dry clay. Washers are glued under the stands to keep the net and hoop from tipping over. The nets are made from a fabric called tulle. It's stapled around the straws.

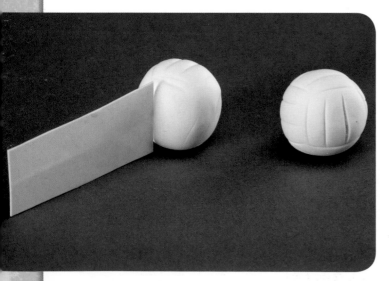

Make A Volleyball

First you'll make a special tool. Think of a volleyball as a cube or a die, with six sides, except the sides are curved. To make a volleyball, first cut a tool from the lid of a cottage cheese or yogurt carton. The width of the tool should be almost as tall as the volleyball.

Mark one section, using the tool to make four up-and-down lines on one side. Mark a second section by turning the tool sideways. Mark four lines, but have the lines go across instead of up and down. Repeat on the third and fourth sides, and then on the top and bottom. Each time the lines will be opposite to the ones next to them. Let the ball dry. As the clay dries, sometimes it will shrink and crack along the lines but that often gives the balls a well worn look.

Make A Soccer Ball

Roll twelve tiny balls because soccer balls have twelve spots on them: one on the top, one on the bottom and two rows of five. Flatten all twelve balls into flat spots. Roll one big ball. Press one spot on top and one on the bottom. Press five spots toward the top in a circle. Press five spots toward the bottom in a circle. Then cut a plastic tool to fit between the spots and press in lines to connect the spots. These lines form triangles.

When you're done, let it dry.

Make Trees For The Park

The trees are made from sticks, air dry clay and heavy metal washers. Poke the sticks into an egg-shaped piece of clay. Glue the clay to a washer and make the leaves from tiny teardrop-shaped pieces of green clay. Glue the leaves to the trees, then let dry.

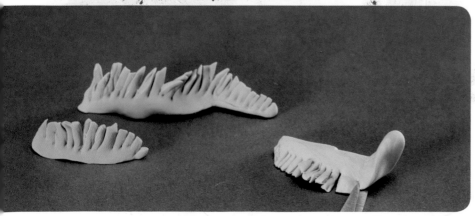

Cut The Grass!

The grass is made from little wedges of clay. Use scissors to clip the grass. Be sure the pieces have a fat bottom so they'll stand up by themselves. Then let dry.

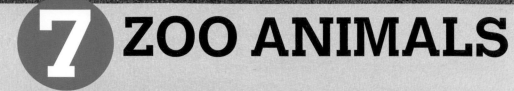

7 ZOO ANIMALS

Each Creature is Unique

In this chapter you'll learn to make a bunch of animals that are very different from each other. Some have an extra-long tail, trunk or neck. Others have a huge mane or very short legs. But they can all be made up of the same essential shapes.

MONKEYS

Body Shapes

Arms, legs and tail — 5 brown ropes

Banana — yellow teardrop

Body — brown teardrop

Ears — flattened beige teardrops

Eyes — 2 black balls and 2 white balls

Face — flattened beige drumstick

Rose — pink rope

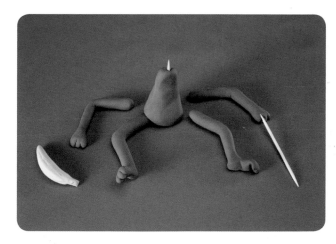

1 MAKE THE BODY PARTS

Make a brown teardrop for the body. To make the hands, flatten the ends of the arm ropes and cut in finger lines. Do the same with the feet but turn up the ends of the legs. Make a heel by using both hands to gently press the clay of the foot and leg together. Cut in lines for toes and one under the toes. For the banana, make a yellow teardrop, then stretch the round end into a point.

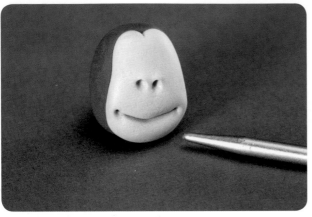

2 **MAKE THE MOUTH AND NOSE**
Press the flattened beige drumstick shape to the front of head. Press in the mouth to make a smile and poke in two holes for a nose.

3 **SHAPE THE EYES AND EARS**
For the eyes, roll two white balls and two slightly smaller black balls. Press on the white ones, then the black ones. Flatten the two teardrop-shaped ears. Press one on each side of the head. Use your thumb to press an indentation in the middle of the ear.

4 **PUT FRIEDA TOGETHER**
Press the legs and arms onto the body, then the rope-shaped tail. Add the head. If you want, put a flower and leaves above one ear and treat the monkey to a banana.

5 **MORE MONKEYS**
Now try putting another monkey together on your own.

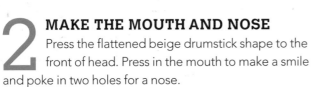

ELEPHANTS

These elephants are a blue-gray color, but you could choose to use a different color of gray. A tiny bit of black added to white will make a charcoal gray color. Some brown mixed in will make a gray-brown color.

Body Shapes

Body — gray egg

Bones — toothpicks

Ears — 2 gray teardrops

Eyes — 2 black balls

Head — gray drumstick

Legs — 4 gray ropes

Tail — yarn or string painted gray

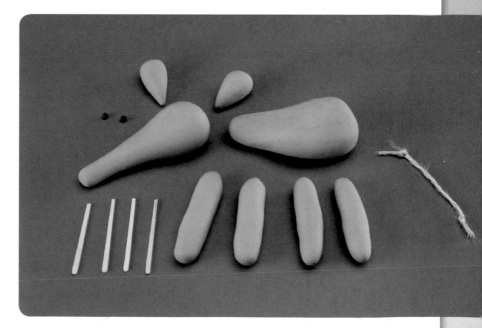

1 SHAPE THE PARTS
These are the shapes that you'll need to make.

2 ADD THE LEGS

To shape the body, turn up the small end of the large, egg-shaped body to make a neck. Insert a toothpick for the neck bone. Press a piece of toothpick into each leg to make them stronger and make sure to shape them. Then press the legs to the sides of the body. This makes the elephant's legs look more powerful. It also makes the body look bigger. And elephants do have big bodies! Poke in a hole for the tail. Prop the body while making the head.

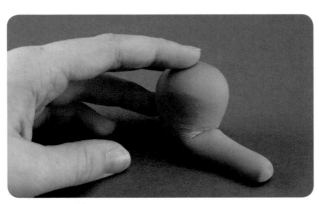

3 MAKE THE HEAD

The front of an elephant's head is a bit flat. Press the long, drumstick-shaped head down against the table to bend the trunk.

4 SHAPE THE TRUNK

To make the trunk longer, roll your finger underneath, where the mouth will be.

5 MAKE THE MOUTH

Use a cut straw tool to press in the mouth. An elephant's mouth is hidden under the trunk.

6 ADD THE HEAD

Add the eyes. Press the head onto the neck. Flatten the teardrop-shaped ears. Press the ears to the sides of the head.

7 PAINT THE TAIL

Use watercolor markers or paint to color the piece of string so the tail matches the body. From clay, make a small teardrop. Make a hole in it. Glue it to the tail.

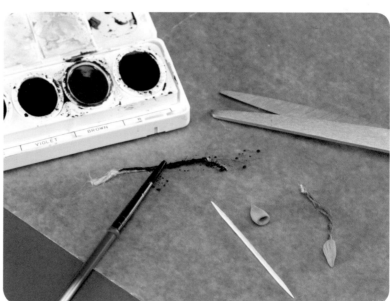

8 ADD THE TAIL

Glue the tail in place.

LIONS

Lions are different from domestic cats in that their muzzles are wider, longer and more powerful looking than those of a cat. A lion has ears that are small and round, while a domestic cat has more pointed ears. But both the lion and the cat have a triangle-shaped nose.

Body Shapes

Body — gold egg

Bones — toothpicks

Ears — 2 flattened gold balls

Eyelids — gold ball cut in half

Eyes — 2 flattened, pale yellow balls, 2 gold balls and 2 black balls

Legs — 4 gold ropes

Mane — multiple flattened gold ropes

Muzzle and chin — 2 gold teardrops and 1 gold ball

Nose — brown ball

Nose ridge — flattened gold drumstick

Tail — gold rope with a teardrop shape at the end

1 MAKE THE BODIES FIRST

The golden yellow color is yellow clay mixed with a little bit of brown clay. Let the bodies dry while you make the heads. It's even better if you can let the bodies dry overnight.

Follow the directions for making a clay cat, but make sure to change the tail. Lions have a tuft on the end of their tails. For the tail, make a rope. Add a teardrop shape to the end. Make hair marks with a toothpick.

2 MAKE THE PARTS FOR THE HEAD

These are the parts that you will need for a lion's head. The size of the head will need to match the size of the body. Try the big head ball on the body to test the size.

3 PUT THE HEAD TOGETHER

Add the ball, for the chin, to the front of the head. Place one of the egg-shaped muzzle pieces on each side of the chin with the small ends touching. Add the eyes in layers, starting with a large pale ball shape. Press a hole in the center of this, then add the golden-brown ball and the black one.

4 ADD THE NOSE RIDGE

This piece adds shape to the lion's head. It starts as a drumstick shape. Flatten it, then press in an indentation on each side so it will fit around the eyes. Press this in place above the muzzle and around the eyes.

5 MAKE THE EYE-LIDS AND NOSE

The eyelids are made from a flattened ball that is cut in half. Press these over the eye. The nose starts as a ball shape. Press in place, then push down to make the top flat. It should look like a triangle.

6 PUT THE PARTS TOGETHER

Add the round ears. Press the head onto the body.

7 ADD A MANE

To make the mane, roll ropes and flatten them. Tear them into small pieces. Press one at a time all around the head.

8 FINISHED

Let the mane dry.

A GIRAFFE

No other animal looks quite like the giraffe — or even similar. Its long neck, long legs and spots are distinctive. However, they have drumstick-shaped heads and ears that stick out to the side like other animals, but both male and female giraffes have short horns.

We're going to make the giraffe lying down because those longs legs and long neck are hard to support with soft clay and toothpicks.

Body Shapes

Body — white drumstick

Bones — toothpicks

Ears — 2 flattened yellow teardrops

Eyelids — flattened yellow ball cut in halves

Eyes — 2 black balls and 2 yellow balls

Head — white drumstick

Horns — 2 white ropes and 2 brown balls

Legs — 4 white ropes

Spots — flattened gold clay or brown and yellow markers

Tail — yellow rope and brown teardrop

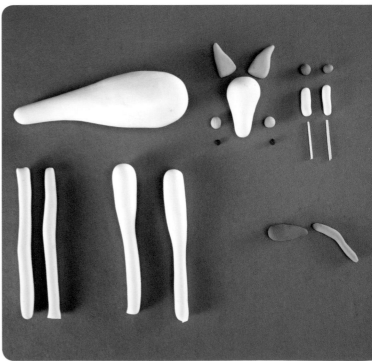

1 MAKE THE SHAPES

These are the shapes that you'll need to make the giraffe.

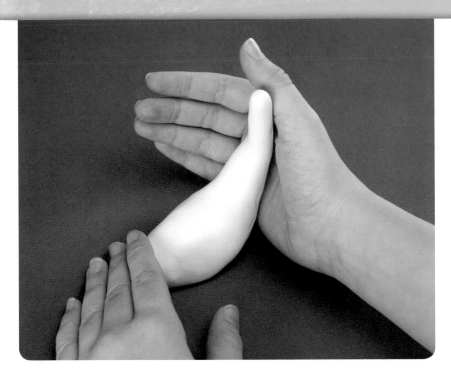

2 MAKE THE BODY

Make a large drumstick shape. Press the neck so it points up from the body.

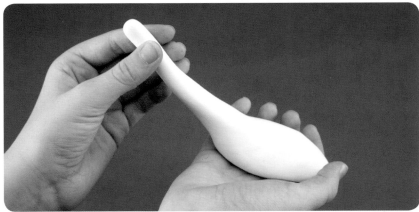

3 MAKE THE NECK

Stretch the neck.

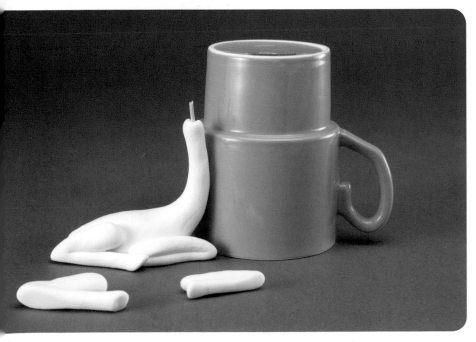

4 MAKE THE LEGS

Add a toothpick to the neck. Lean it against something to support it while you make the legs. Roll ropes for the legs. The front legs are thinner than the back legs, and the back legs are wider at the top.

Press the bottoms of the feet against the table to make them flat where their hooves would be. Bend all four legs at the knee. Notice that the front and back legs bend in opposite directions. Press the legs against the body.

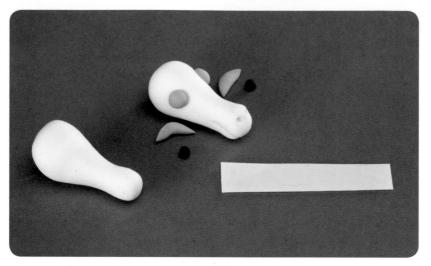

5 MAKE THE HEAD

The head is a long drumstick shape. Cut the mouth line. Poke in nostrils. Add yellow and black balls for the eyes. The eyelids are a flat circle cut in half and then shaped with points at the corners.

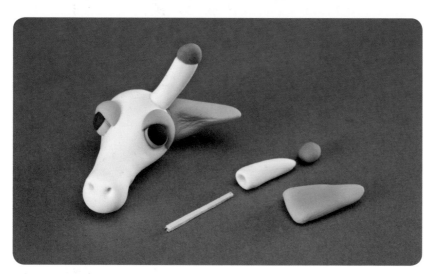

6 ADD THE EARS AND HORNS

To make the horns, roll two short ropes. Insert a short piece of toothpick into each horn. Add a brown ball on top. To make the ears, roll two teardrop shapes. Press the horns in place, then add the ears. Use a paintbrush handle to indent the center of the ears.

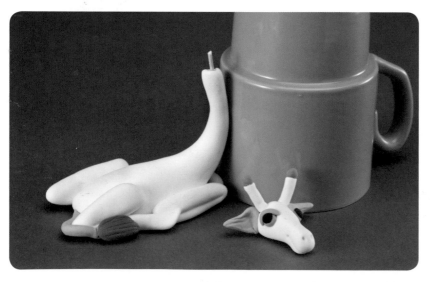

7 ADD THE TAIL

The tail is a rope shape. Add a brown teardrop shape to the end. Make lines in the teardrop to look like hair. Put the head onto the neck. Prop until dry.

8 MAKE THE SPOTS

Once dry, add the spots. Some spots are made from flattened, irregular pieces of golden-colored clay that are pressed onto the body. Other spots are made with a brown watercolor marker.

PENGUINS

These two little penguins are modeled after Gentoo Penguins, which are one of sixteen different species of penguins in the world. I chose to make this penguin because I like the orange beak and feet. Not all penguins have orange as one of their main colors.

If you look up penguins you'll see that the Gentoo Penguin has a longer body and smaller head than these clay ones. The adults also have a white stripe that goes across the top of their heads. I've made some exaggerations when making these little clay penguins. That's part of the fun of creating clay animals— you can make changes, you don't have to copy exactly. Look at the pictures or the real animal just to get ideas.

Body Shapes

Back feathers — flattened black egg

Beak — orange teardrop

Body — white egg

Chest strip — black rope

Eyebrows — white rope

Eyes — 2 large black balls, 2 small black balls and 2 tiny white balls

Feet — 2 flattened orange teardrops

Head — black egg

Stripes — flattened black rope

Tail — flattened black egg

Wings — 2 flattened, black teardrops and 2 flattened, white teardrops

1 MAKE THE BODY SHAPES

Roll a white egg shape for the main body piece. Make two black egg shapes, one for the tail and one for the back. Roll a short black rope to go across the chest. Flatten all three pieces.

2 ADD THE BODY PIECES AND MAKE FEET

Press the flat black egg shape across the penguin's back. Add the tail and the black strip across the chest.

To make feet, roll two orange teardrop shapes. Flatten them. Press under the body and use a toothpick to mark toe lines.

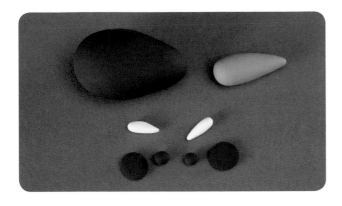

3 MAKE THE HEAD PIECES
Role the clay to make the head and face features.

4 MAKE A HOLE FOR THE BEAK
Use a knitting needle or paintbrush handle to make a hole in the head where the beak will go.

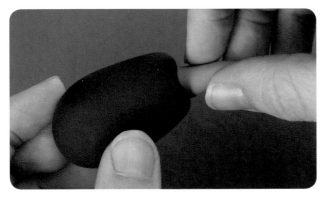

5 ATTACH THE BEAK
Press the beak into the hole.

6 DETAIL THE BEAK AND MAKE THE FACE
Cut a line across the beak on both sides. Smooth the black clay around the beak. Make a hole in the head where the eyes will go. Press in the large black ball. Make another hole. Press in the small black ball. To add the highlight to the eyeball, add the tiny white ball to the side of the eye. Press the white stripe above the eye.

7 ADD THE WINGS
The wings are each made from two flattened teardrop shapes. Make the black one bigger than the white one. Press the two wing pieces together. Press the wings to the side of the body. The Gentoo Penguin has a black stripe beside each wing. Make this stripe with a short, flattened rope.

A Sleuth of Bears
A SIMPLE BEAR

By looking at this simple little bear, we can see that bears have a round black nose, like dogs. Their eyes are in the front of their face, like the eyes of people, cats, dogs and raccoons. Their ears are round, like mouse ears, though their ears don't look oversized in proportion to their heads like mouse ears sometimes do. Bear ears are much smaller.

Body Shapes

Body — brown egg

Ears — 2 brown balls

Eyes — 2 black balls

Front legs or arms — long brown rope that is bigger at both ends, like 2 drumsticks put together

Head — brown ball

Neck bone — toothpick

Nose — black ball

Snout or muzzle — brown teardrop

1 MAKE THE BODY
Press the toothpick into the egg shape. Lay the arm piece around the back of the neck. Bring the two ends to the front to make arms and paws. The extra clay behind the neck will make the bear look stronger. This is one of the things that we notice about bears. Their bodies are thick.

2 MAKE THE HEAD
To make the snout, press the teardrop shape to the front of the head toward the bottom. Make the mouth. Add the black ball nose and the eyes. Flatten the ear balls a bit, then press them into place.

A POLAR BEAR

Plan to make the polar bear in two stages. First you'll make the bare body without fur. Let this dry overnight; then add the fur the next day. That way you can press quite hard with the toothbrush without smashing the shape of the body.

Look at the body shape. Bears often hold their heads out and down from the body, not up like a dog's head. They'll sit up or stand on their back legs to get a good look around. A bear's body often shows a hump in the middle of the back.

Body Shapes

Body — white drumstick

Bones — toothpicks

Eyes/nose — 3 black balls

Fur — flattened white clay

Legs — 4 drumsticks

Tail — white teardrop

1 MAKE THE BODY SHAPE

Start the body as a long egg shape. Turn it into a drumstick shape. Now shape the snout with your fingers. It's pointed. Press the back so there is a hump. Make a slope from the hump toward the tail.

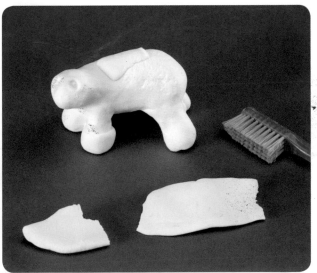

3 ADD FUR

After the body is dry, add the fur. To make the fur, flatten white clay. Press the flat clay over the body, covering all of the hardened body, head and legs. Use a toothbrush to press a furry texture into the surface. Add the nose, eyes, ears and tail.

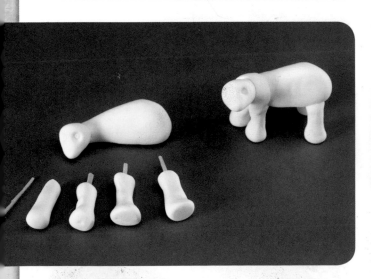

2 MAKE LEGS

Form legs into short drumstick shapes. Put a piece of toothpick into each. Press the legs into the body. Let dry overnight.

A PANDA BEAR

Panda bears have distinctive black and white markings. To keep the black clay from smearing onto the white clay, roll all of the white parts first and then make the black ones.

Body Shapes

Back legs — 2 black drumsticks

Black stripe around body — black rope long enough to stretch around chest

Body — white egg

Ears — 2 small black balls

Eye circles — 2 medium-sized black balls, flattened to circles

Eyes — 2 tiny black balls

Front legs — 2 black balls rolled into small ropes

Head — white ball

Neck bone — toothpick

Nose — black ball

Snout or muzzle — white egg

1 MAKE BODY SHAPES

Roll each piece of clay into the right size and shape for each of the bear's body parts.

2 SHAPE THE LEGS AND ADD DETAILS

Shape the legs like long drumsticks. Turn up the bottom of the front legs to make a paw. Turn up the bottom of the back legs to make a foot shape. Use a toothpick to press in the lines between the toes. Press in some lines underneath the toes. Put in a toothpick for the neck bone. To make a stripe around the body, flatten a large rope, then press it around the body. Press the legs in place.

3 MAKE THE FACE

Press the snout to the head. Place eye circles above the snout. Poke in holes for the eyes. Add black eyes. Press on the ears. Roll the nose ball into an oval shape, then indent the center with a finger to make it bowed. Press the nose in place. Use a toothpick to poke a hole into the center of each eye.

4 ATTACH THE HEAD

Press the head onto the body.

Let's Look at Eyes

Noticing details is something that artists learn very early. They learn to see things. They pay attention. So look at some pictures of a rabbit, a mouse, a chipmunk and a raccoon to use as a reference tool. You might notice that their ears are all different, but what about their eyes?

I'm guessing that you saw a number of things, but one thing that rabbits, mice and chipmunks have in common is that their eyes are toward the sides of their heads. It's their most distinctive feature. Pictures of these animals often show them looking toward you with just one eye showing. The raccoon is different, though. The raccoon's eyes are in the front of the face just like the eyes of cats, dogs, bears and monkeys.

In cartoons of rabbits, chipmunks or mice, you'll often see that the artist has chosen to put the eyes on the front of the face. That's because it makes them look friendlier. It's also easier to give expression to their faces when we can see both eyes.

In the projects in this chapter, notice where the eyes are placed. Experiment. Make yours different from mine. Maybe you like them funnier or scarier or with big features, like in cartoons. There are many ways to make the same animal. What's important is that you see the differences and that you choose how you want to make it.

Body Shapes

Arms — 2 long brown eggs

Body — brown egg shape

Ear bones — 2 toothpicks

Ears — 2 flattened brown eggs

Eyes — 2 tiny black balls

A SIMPLE RABBIT

1 The rabbit's body starts just like the cat's or the dog's — as an egg.

2 To give a little shape to the head, roll your finger right under that place where the chin might be. Use a toothpick, straw tools and tiny plastic tools to press in the eyes and the mouth and nose lines. Flatten two long eggs for the ears. Put a piece of toothpick into each ear. Press the ears into the head.

3 Press in black balls for the eyes. Press on the ears. Roll two long eggs for arms. Press the long egg-shaped arms in place. Bend the body or keep it standing straight.

A Look at Noses and Ears

You can use the same basic egg shape as the body for most of your clay animals. But pay attention to the differences in the nose and ear shapes. If you do, you'll be able to create a whole collection of cute critters.

So far in this book we've made a ball and triangle nose for the cats, a black ball nose for the dogs and a V-shaped mark for the rabbit's nose. Now how about the mouse?

If you're familiar with cartoon mice and their noses, you may think that mouse noses are black, but they usually aren't. The round black noses in cartoons are choices that particular artists made when deciding how to draw or sculpt a mouse. In real mice, the noses are often pink at the end, or sometimes they're just brown, like the fur.

A SITTING MOUSE

Body Shapes

Ears — 2 flattened, pale pink-brown balls

Eyes — 2 tiny black balls

Feet — 4 pink teardrops

Head — a long brown egg or teardrop shape

Tail — brown painted rope or string

1 MAKE THE BODY

Roll a long egg or teardrop shape for the head and body. Then bend the top over to make the face and nose. The ears on a mouse are often a light pink, so mix together pink, white and brown to make a pale pink-brown color.

2 MAKE THE HEAD
Bend the top of the teardrop over to create the head. If the nose isn't pointed, use your fingers to gently roll it into a soft point.

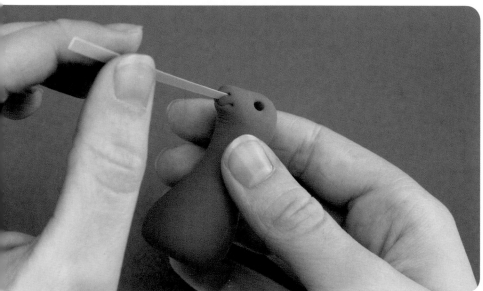

3 MAKE THE MOUTH AND NOSE
If your mouse is tiny, you'll need really small tools to cut in the nose and mouth lines. I used tools that were cut from a tiny straw and a thin plastic deli lid. The shape of the nose looks a lot like the rabbit's, but this nose is much more pointed. Press in the eyes on the sides of the head.

4 MAKE THE EARS
Mouse ears are round and quite big in comparison to the head. Roll two pink balls and flatten them.

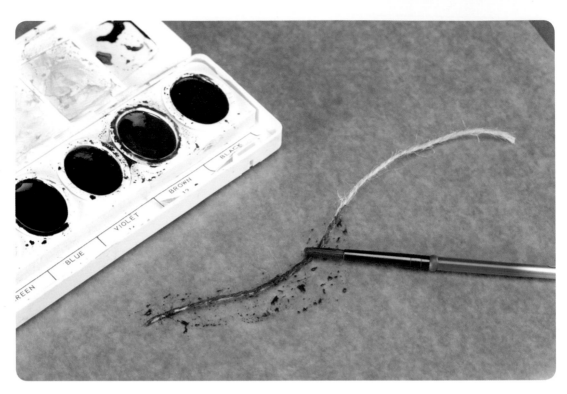

5 MAKE THE TAIL

A mouse tail is a very skinny rope. If we made this from clay, it would most likely break, so we'll use a piece of string. If you don't have brown string, paint it with your watercolor paints and let it dry.

6 ADD THE EARS AND TAIL

Press the ears in place. Make a hole in the back side of the mouse for the tail. Glue the tail into the hole.

A WALKING MOUSE

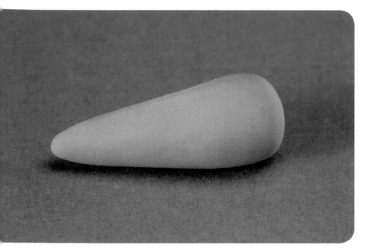

1 SHAPE THE BODY
Begin with the same shape you used for the previous mouse but lay the teardrop shape down.

2 SHAPE THE NECK
Roll your finger across the neck area to indent the teardrop. Roll balls for ears and eyes.

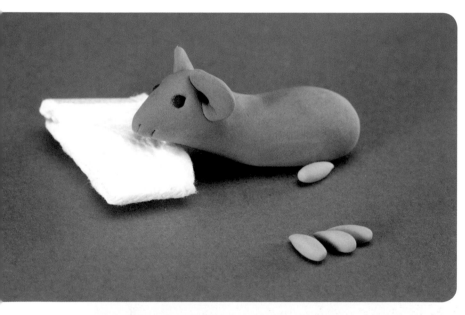

3 FINISH THE HEAD AND MAKE FEET
Make the face and ears just like you did for the previous clay mouse. If you like, add a little pink paint to the nose. Prop the head up. Roll four pink teardrops for feet. Press the feet under the body with just the toes showing.

4 MAKE THE TOES
Use a plastic tool to cut lines between the toes. Glue the tail in place. Let it dry.

Make More Detailed Feet

What's unique about this rabbit is its more detailed feet. And once you learn to make these feet, you might use similar feet for a cat, bear or raccoon. Until then, you could add even more detail by adding toe pads on the bottom side. Look up some pictures of animal feet for more ideas.

Body Shapes

Arms — 2 small, pink drumsticks

Body — pink egg

Ear bones — 2 toothpicks

Ears — 2 flattened, pink teardrops

Eyelids — 2 pink teardrops

Eyes — 2 tiny black balls, 2 slightly bigger blue balls and 2 slightly bigger white balls

Head — pink egg

Leaves — green teardrops

Legs — 2 pink drumsticks

Neck bone — toothpick

Roses — red ropes

Tail — white ball

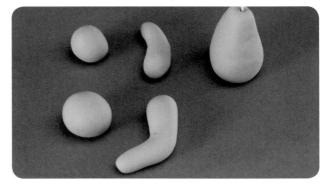

1 MAKE THE BODY AND LEGS

For the body, make an egg shape. Then add a toothpick for the neck bone, roll a ball for each arm and leg, and form them into drumstick shapes. Make sure the legs are bigger than the arms.

2 FORM THE HEEL

On the legs, form the foot and heel by using both hands to gently press the clay toward the heel. Pat the heel smooth with your fingers.

3 MARK THE TOES

Use a toothpick to mark in lines for the toes.

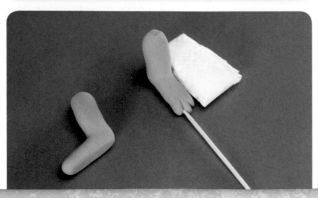

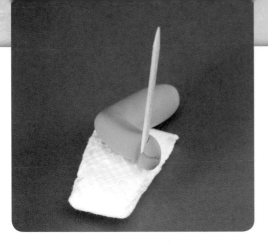

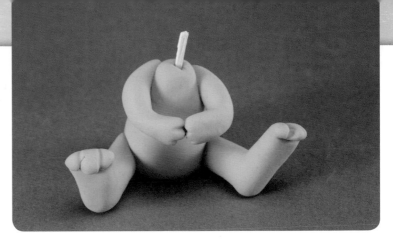

4 CURVE THE TOES

To make the toes curve, bend them over the toothpick.

5 ADD ARMS AND LEGS

Mark finger lines on the arms. Press the arms and legs to the body.

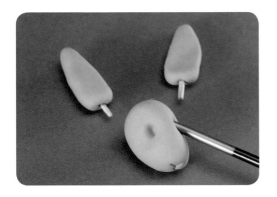

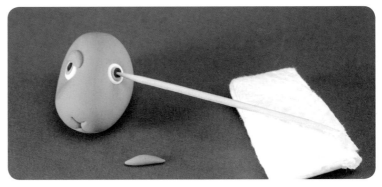

6 MAKE THE HEAD AND EARS

Roll an egg shape for the head. Make the face using plastic tools to cut the mouth and nose lines. Make holes for eye sockets. For ears, roll two teardrop shapes, then flatten them. Press in a piece of toothpick for support.

7 ADD THE EYES AND EYELIDS

Roll a white, blue and black ball for each eye. Keep the black balls very small! Press the eye balls into the sockets, one color at a time. Poke a hole in the center. For the eyelid, roll a ball, then use your finger to roll against one side of the ball to make a pointed teardrop shape. Repeat on the other side. Press this double teardrop over the eye.

8 MAKE ROSES

To make roses, roll small ropes. Flatten them and roll them up loosely. Pinch and pull the back sides into a stem shape. Use your finger to turn down the edges of the petals. Make at least five roses. Imagine that they smell wonderful!

9 MAKE LEAVES

To make leaves, roll balls then teardrops. Press them flat and press center with a toothpick to make a vein line.

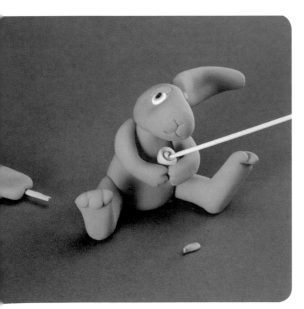

10 PUT IT ALL TOGETHER

Finish the rabbit up and add a bouquet. Add the head and ears. Use a toothpick to pick up the leaves and flowers and press them into the hands and between the ears, place little accent balls of different colors. And don't forget to add the tail!

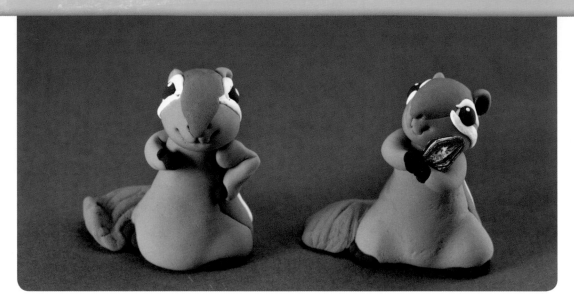

Add Stripes

Animals usually aren't just one color. Sometimes they have stripes or spots. These chipmunks have three stripes down their backs and one above and one below each eye. What is the easiest way to add these stripes? Let's make them and find out.

CHIPMUNKS

1 MEASURE OUT YOUR COLORS

These are the colors that you'll need for the chipmunks. Roll the egg shapes for the head and body, plus the two ropes for the arms, before you start adding any stripes. That way if you run out of the light brown color before you finish all four pieces, you can start over, making smaller pieces.

Body Shapes

Arms — 2 short brown ropes

Back fur — flattened, dark brown egg shape

Body — brown egg

Eyes — 2 flattened white circles, 2 black balls and 2 tiny, flattened, white circles

Feet/hands — 4 black eggs

Head — brown egg

Head fur — flattened, dark brown teardrop

Neck bone — toothpick

Seeds — ropes of black and white clay

Stripes — flattened white ropes

Tail — brown teardrop

2 SHAPE THE BODY

Roll an egg shape for the body. Press in a toothpick for the neck bone. To shape the leg area, press your thumb against each side of the belly.

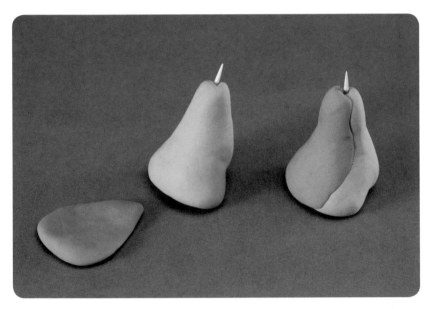

3 ADD DARKER FUR

From the dark brown clay, roll a large egg shape. Flatten it. Press it over the back.

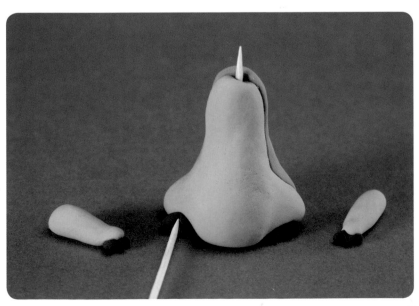

4 MAKE HIS ARMS AND FEET

To make the arms, roll two short ropes. For the feet and hands, roll four small black egg shapes. Press two feet under the hips and two hands onto each arm. Use a toothpick to mark in finger lines.

5 MAKE THE HEAD

For the head, roll an egg shape. Roll a long teardrop shape. Flatten it. Lay it over the top of the head from the tip of the nose to back of the head.

6 MAKE THE FACE

Use a straw tool, a piece of cut plastic and a toothpick to make the mouth and nose. To make the eyes, add a flat white circle where the eye will be. Press a hole in the center then push in two black balls. Add the tiny flattened white balls to the black balls in order to complete the eyes.

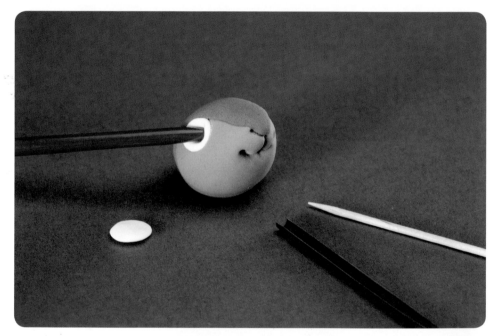

7 MAKE THE STRIPES

For the stripes, roll long, skinny ropes. Press short pieces over and under each eye. Press one stripe down the middle of the back. Press a long stripe from the corner of the eye all the way down the back. Do this on both sides.

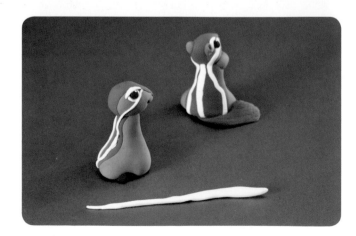

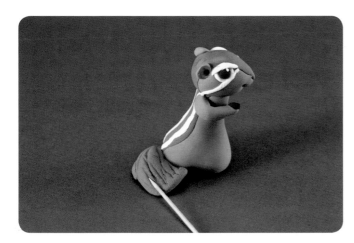

8 ADD THE ARMS AND TAIL

Press on the arms. For the tail, roll a large teardrop shape. Flatten it. Press in place. Use a toothpick to draw in hair lines.

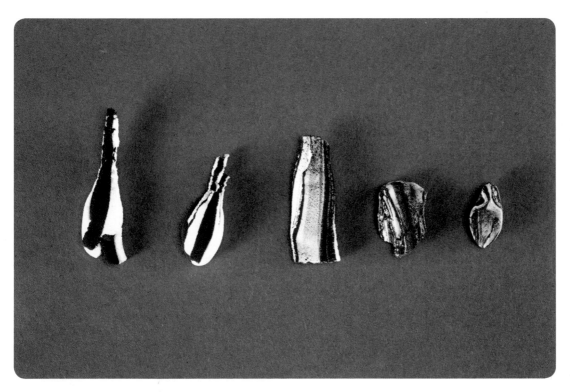

9 MAKE THE SUNFLOWER SEEDS

Roll several small, short ropes of black and white clay. Lay them next to each other. Stretch the ropes, then break them into pieces and stack together. Stretch again. Break into pieces and stack again. Repeat until the stripes are quite small. Cut into small pieces. Form pieces into sunflower shapes.

Build a Face With Layers

RACCOONS

When you make these lively raccoons, you'll get to practice almost everything you've learned so far in this book. These raccoons have marbled fur, stripes and spots. Their faces are made from several shapes put together in layers. Plus their fur has texture. Are you ready? You'll need brown, white and black clay. A raccoon's fur isn't a solid color, so you'll mix the three colors together for parts of the fur.

Body Shapes

Arms — brown mix, 2 curved teardrops

Back legs — brown mix, 2 medium-sized teardrops

Body and head — brown mix, a short drumstick

Ears — brown mix, 2 small eggs

Face — 2 black teardrops for cheeks, 2 white circles for eye mask, 1 white teardrop for muzzle, 1 white teardrop for hair on top of head, 2 black balls for eyes and 1 black ball for the nose

Feet and paws — 4 small, black eggs

Tail — fat brown rope and skinny black and white ropes

1 MIX COLORS FOR FUR
To make the slightly striped, marbled color for the raccoon's fur, mix together brown, white and black clay. Roll it into a rope. Flatten, stretch and break the strip in half. Put the two halves together and repeat. Do this until the color mix is slightly marbled but all three colors still show.

2 MAKE THE SHAPES
Twist, twirl and roll the clay into the shapes you need.

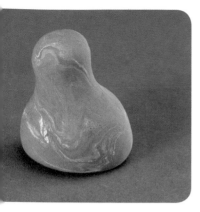

3 MAKE THE BODY

Start with the body and head shape as one piece.

4 MAKE THE FACE

Push the two flat white circles onto the face where the eyes will be. Add the muzzle, which is the large white teardrop shape. Push into the face with an old toothbrush to make marks for hair texture.

5 ADD BLACK CLAY

Flatten the two black teardrops for the cheeks. Lay the small part of each teardrop under where the eyes will be. Press the teardrops down on each side of the nose. Add the white teardrop to the top of the head.

6 MAKE THE EYES, MOUTH AND EARS

Press in holes for the eyes. Make the mouth. Position the ears. Use a paintbrush handle to push the ears down onto the head. Add the balls for the nose and eyes. Notice the tiny white ball for the highlight in the eyes.

7 ATTACH THE PAWS

Attach the paws and feet to the arms and legs. Raccoons use their paws like hands, so they'll need lines cut for their fingers and toes!

8 MAKE THE TAIL

Twist ropes of black, brown and white clay together. Add more strips of black or white clay as needed. Press the tail to the body.

The Same but Different

SHEEP

Body Shapes

Body — white and black drumsticks

Bones — 10 toothpicks

Ears — 4 white teardrops

Eyelids — 1 black, flat circle cut in half and 1 white, flat circle cut in half

Eyes — 2 black balls, 2 yellow balls, 2 tiny black balls

Head — white and black drumsticks

Legs — 4 black ropes and 4 white ropes

Tail — 2 white balls

Wool — multiple small white balls

1 DIFFERENT WOOL
These sheep have the same body shape but their wool is attached in different ways. Their legs and faces are different colors, too.

2 MAKE THEIR BODIES AND HEADS
Their heads, bodies and legs are very much like the ponies that you'll see in the next chapter. But the sheep's mouths and noses look more like the mouth and nose of the rabbits. The nostrils are also more like slits. Create the bodies and let them dry overnight before adding the wool.

3 MAKE CURLY WOOL
Cover the sheep's thoroughly dried body with strips of white clay. Don't add any new clay to the legs or face.

4 MAKE CURLS
While the clay is still soft, use a pointed tool like a knitting needle to make little twisting curls all over the body.

5 ADD EARS AND TAIL

The ears, which are teardrop shaped, fit on the sides of the head. They point out to the side. Press them in place with a paintbrush handle. Then add a tail.

6 ADD BUMPY WOOL

Be sure that the body is thoroughly dry. For this wool, add flat sheets of white clay all over the body and the top of the head. Don't cover the black face and legs.

7 ROLL LOTS AND LOTS OF BALLS

The wool is made by pressing balls of white clay all over the layers of white clay.

8 FINISHING TOUCHES

Add the ears.

How to Turn Your Treasures Into Sculpture

There are so many fantasy elements that come to life while walking outside. The possibilities for sculptures are endless.

STONE SCULPTURES

Repairs

If your rock sculptures come apart after they dry, use glue to put them back together.

1 STACK THE ROCKS

Stack some rocks and make them stick together by pressing some brown air dry clay between them. Press firmly so it sticks. Add texture to the clay, if you like, by tapping it with one of the rough rocks or the acorn cap.

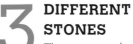

2 ADD STICKS

Add sticks to turn it into a rock man.

3 DIFFERENT STONES

These two sculptures were made from different collections of stones. The stone that was used for the dog's face was a terrific find, so all I added was the nose and the ears. The legs and tail are air dry clay.

A Fairy

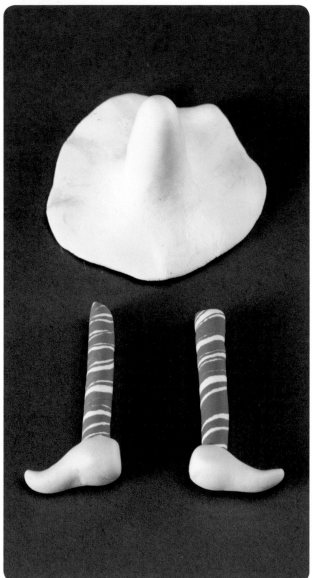

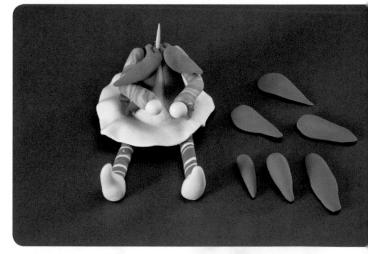

1 MAKE THE DRESS, LEGS AND SHOES

Choose whatever colors you like for this project. Begin the dress with an egg shape. Press down on the egg to flatten the big end and turn it into a cone shape. Stretch the bottom edge of the cone to create a ruffled skirt. To make legs, twist two colors together to make a striped rope. Cut two pieces. Make fairy shoes from two egg shapes. Roll the small end of the shoes into a point. Make a hole in the center of the shoes and press in the legs.

2 MAKE A FAIRY SHIRT COVERED IN PETALS

To make petals, start with seven to ten small balls of clay. Roll balls into teardrop shapes, then flatten into petal shapes. Press five or six petals around the top of the dress. Make arms from striped clay. Add hands and press a toothpick into the top of the body. Press arms near the top of the dress by toothpick. Finish by adding small petals around the toothpick to make a collar. Poke two holes into the back for the wings.

3 FREDDIE THE SNAIL

Choose a small snail shell or seashell from your collection. Roll a small egg, then stretch the small end to create a neck. Press the snail into the shell. Now it'll be easier to hold. Use a straw tool to cut in the mouth. To make the snail smile more, poke the corners of the mouth with a toothpick. To make the eyes, poke them in with the tip of a black marker. Fit the snail into the fairy's arms.

4 MAKE SEED POD FAIRY WINGS

Collect seed pods from a maple, box elder or linden tree. Place wax paper under the seeds, then paint them using yellow watercolor paint. Let dry. Spread gold glitter glue over one side of the wings. Let dry. Then use glitter glue on the other side and poke the wings into the holes in the back of the dress.

A Seashell Mermaid

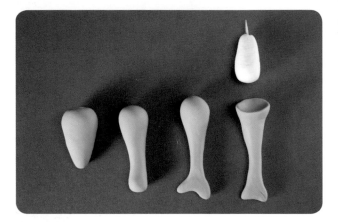

1 MAKE THE BODY PARTS

Roll a large green egg shape and a smaller flesh-colored egg shape. Press a toothpick into the smaller egg. Roll the green egg into a longer egg. Continue rolling and stretching until it is quite long. Press the small end flat. Shape a notch in the small end of the tail so it looks like a fish tail. Use your fingers or a round tool to open up a hole in the large end.

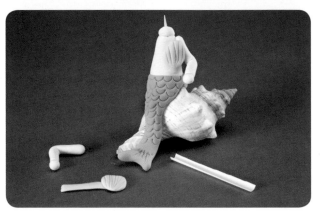

2 PRESS TOGETHER

Press the body and tail pieces together, then set on the shell. Use your straw tool to press in scale marks. Make arms, then press them into place. Add a neck. Create a shell top from two flattened egg shapes. Press in lines. Add a small flat piece to connect the two shells.

3 PUT ON THE HEAD

Make the head. Press it in place. Style the hair from long ropes of clay. Make a little book or some other treasure to put in the mermaid's hands. Let everything dry.

Materials

A shell that looks like it might be a mermaid throne

Air dry clay for a tail, skin, a shell top, hair and a book for her hands

Beads for eyes

Glitter glue

Toothpick

Pinecone Owls

There are so many shapes of pinecones. Collect a bunch, then sort through them to find the best ones to turn into owl bodies.

1 MAKE WINGS

Make wings from flattened egg or teardrop shapes. Add feather marks with the straw tool. Press the wings to the pinecone.

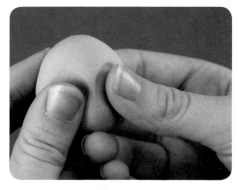

2 MAKE THE HEAD

Roll a ball for the head. Use your thumbs to press in eye sockets.

3 MAKE THE FACE

Press the head onto the pinecone. Add eyes made from three different sized balls of clay: one white, one orange and one black. Add a black teardrop-shaped beak. If you want your owls to look like a Great Horned Owl or a Screech Owl, add the V-shaped piece over their eyes.

Tip

Some pinecones will stand up on their own. If they don't, add some air dry clay to the bottom to help support them, then let them dry.

A String of Ponies

All ponies are built with the same basic body shape. It's the finishing touches of manes, horns or wings that make each one distinctive. So, you'll make this project in two parts. First you'll make the body and legs. Let them dry overnight. Then add the rest of the parts. This will help the legs keep their shape.

A SIMPLE PONY

This simple pony has clay body parts, but the mane and tail are made from yarn. If you don't have yarn, you can use strips of clay to make the mane and tail.

Body Shapes

Body — brown drumstick

Bones — 5 toothpicks

Ears — 2 brown teardrops

Eyelids — 1 brown, flat circle cut in half

Eyes — 2 black balls

Head — brown drumstick

Legs — 4 brown ropes

Mane and tail — yarn

Spots — flattened white clay

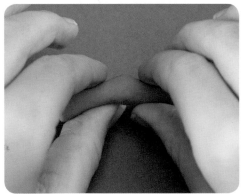

1 SHAPE KNEES
To make legs, roll ropes. For the knees, use both hands to roll the middle of the leg between your fingers. This will create a bulge for the knee.

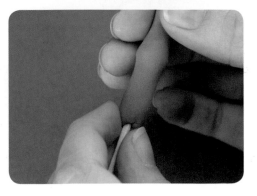

2 SHAPE THE HOOVES
To make sure this pony has strong legs, press a toothpick into each leg. Reshape the knee if you need to do so. To shape the hoof, use your fingers to smooth and flatten the front foot.

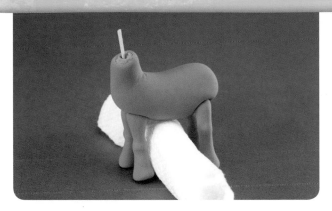

3 MAKE THE BODY AND LET DRY

For the body, make a drumstick shape. Turn up the small end to make a neck. Insert a toothpick for the neck bone. Press in the legs. Make a hole for the tail pieces to fit into. Prop and let dry overnight so the body gets very firm.

4 MAKE THE HEAD

Make a drumstick shape for the head. Try it on the body to see if you like the size. Use a plastic cutting tool or knife to cut in the mouth. Poke holes for the nostrils and eyes. Press the head to the body.

6 FINISH THE HEAD

Add eyes and half circles for eyelids. For ears, roll teardrop shapes. Flatten and press them into place, and make sure they point up. Use a paintbrush handle to make the hole in the center of the ears.

5 ADD SPOTS

Press irregular, flat, white shapes all over the body and head.

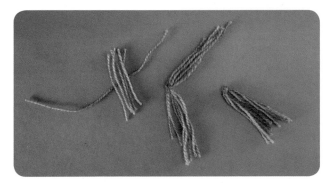

7 MAKE THE MANE AND TAIL

To make the mane and tail, cut pieces of yarn twice the length that you'd like the mane or tail to be. Lay these pieces on a longer piece of yarn. Use the long piece of yarn to tie across the center of the pieces. Tie tightly with a knot. You now have a tassel. Make one for the mane and one for the tail and, if you like, add more.

8 GLUE IN PLACE

Glue short pieces of yarn between the ears to make a fringe. Glue on the tassel to create the mane. Fit the tail into the hole, then glue in place.

A GLAMOROUS PONY

Have you ever noticed in parades how some horses have their hair braided? Let's use those trendy horses as our reference for a glamour pony.

Body Shapes

Body — black drumstick

Bones — 5 toothpicks

Ears — 2 black teardrops

Eyelids — 1 black, flat circle cut in half

Eyes — 2 black balls

Head — black drumstick

Legs — 4 black ropes

Mane and tail — black and blue twisted ropes

Rose — flattened, blue rope

1 ADD A CLAY MANE

Make the body and head the same as you did for the simple pony. Let the body and legs dry overnight, then add the head. The mane and tail are thin ropes that are twisted, then pressed in place with a toothpick.

2 ADD RIBBONS AND THE ROSE

For ribbons, roll thin clay ropes. Flatten the ropes, then twist them. Press in place with a toothpick if you can. Twist some black and blue ropes together before you add them.

To make the rose, roll a long, flat strip of blue clay. Roll it up very loosely, then pinch the bottom. Use your finger to curl the edges of the petals. Press onto the ribbons.

3 ADD GLITTER

In this picture, the pony has three colors of glitter glue applied to the ribbons, rose and eyelids. Let the glue dry thoroughly.

A UNICORN

There can't be other fantasy animals in this chapter without including a mythological unicorn. Their tales are as old as time.

1 REPEAT PREVIOUS STEPS

Create this unicorn by using the directions for the glamorous pony, but use white clay instead of black. Make the horn by wrapping a strip of white clay around a toothpick. Spread white or clear glitter glue on the horn. Let it dry. Cut off most of the toothpick. Press the horn into the forehead.

2 ADD THE REST OF THE GLAMOUR

Be sure the legs and body are thoroughly dry before adding the mane and tail. Make the mane and tail pieces from white clay ropes. Make pink twisted ribbons from pink clay ropes. Make leaves from flattened teardrop shapes. Roll up a flattened rope to make the roses. Add these pieces a few at a time, poking them in place with a toothpick. Put the glitter glue on last then let everything dry thoroughly.

A PEGASUS

Make the body just like you made the unicorn's, but cut two slits where the wings will fit.

Body Shapes

Body — white egg

Bones — tooth-picks

Eyes — 2 black balls

Legs — 4 white ropes

Tail and mane — multicolored yarn or string

Wings — colored or painted card-stock

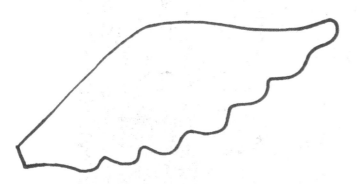

1 MAKE THE BODY AND THE WING PATTERN

While the body is drying, make the mane, tail and wings. Cut and tie yarn to make tassels for the mane and tail, just like the ones you did for the simple pony.

Copy the wing pattern onto cardstock or heavy white paper. You'll need two wings.

2 ADD COLOR AND GLITTER GLUE

Cut out the wings. Decorate one side with watercolor markers. Let dry, then decorate the other side. Add glitter glue. Let dry.

3 ADD THE MANE, TAIL AND WINGS

Glue the mane and tail pieces in place. Poke the wings into the slots. If the paper is too soft, you can glue a small piece of flat toothpick to the back side of the wings. Let dry, then add the wings to the body.

About the Author

Ever since Maureen can remember, she has been making things. Her mother made sure that there were always art supplies around and that there were books and pets and things to discover. Her family lived on a farm with a big garden next to the woods. Oftentimes things that they grew or found on hikes became her art materials. This taught her to look at life through curious eyes. Thanks to those early years, Maureen knows that there is always something to do, something to explore, something to create. She says she will never be able to do all of the things on her lists because, of course, they are always expanding. And about that she feels very lucky!

Maureen is an author, teacher, Storyclay Teller, artist and retreat facilitator. Her previous books with F+W include *How to Make Clay Characters* and *Clay Characters for Kids*, both published by North Light Books. In 1998 she and husband, Dan, opened Maureen Carlson's Center for Creative Arts in Jordan, Minnesota. For more info, see WeeFolk.com or MaureenCarlson.com.

Metric Conversion Chart

To convert	to	multiply by
Inches	Centimeters	2.54
Centimeters	Inches	0.4
Feet	Centimeters	30.5
Centimeters	Feet	0.03
Yards	Meters	0.9
Meters	Yards	1.1

Other fine IMPACT Books are available from your favorite bookstore, art supply store or online supplier. Visit our website at fwmedia.com.

18 17 16 15 14   5 4 3 2 1

DISTRIBUTED IN CANADA BY FRASER DIRECT
100 Armstrong Avenue
Georgetown, ON, Canada L7G 5S4
Tel: (905) 877-4411

DISTRIBUTED IN THE U.K. AND EUROPE
BY F&W MEDIA INTERNATIONAL LTD
Brunel House, Forde Close, Newton Abbot, TQ12 4PU, UK
Tel: (+44) 1626 323200, Fax: (+44) 1626 323319
Email: enquiries@fwmedia.com

DISTRIBUTED IN AUSTRALIA BY CAPRICORN LINK
P.O. Box 704, S. Windsor NSW, 2756 Australia
Tel: (02) 4560-1600; Fax: (02) 4577 5288
Email: books@capricornlink.com.au

ISBN 13: 978-1-4403-3635-5

Edited by Brittany VanSnepson and Vanessa Wieland
Designed by Bethany Rainbolt
Photography by Christine Polomsky
Production coordinated by Mark Griffin
Hand modeling by Erin Barker

Acknowledgments

How many people does it really take to create a book like this? Even though I've been writing how-to books since 1991, I didn't even begin to understand how many individual talents were involved until I went to the F+W offices to do the photo shoot for this book. Thank you ALL!

A special bow to Brittany VanSnepson and Vanessa Wieland, editors, and Christine Polomsky, photographer, who turned what could have been a stressful time into one that was thoroughly joyful. And a round of applause for the hand model, Erin, who hung in there for a long day of hand shots. Bravo!

Meanwhile, back at the Center for Creative Arts, it was Renee Carlson who picked up the slack and saw that things did, indeed, get done.

Dedication

For Renee, who has been on this creative journey with me since she was a little girl. Thanks to her, these books did get done! Her memories of what she loved when she was a little girl are part of the inspiration for these books. I can still picture her as a 10 year old making little plates of clay cookies to sell in our booth at the Minnesota Renaissance Festival. During the making of these books, she created both clay food and real food and picked up the pieces when I got too busy to see through the piles. Thank you!

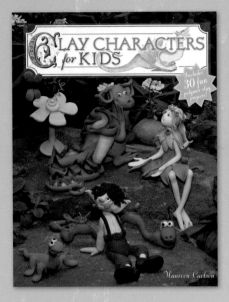
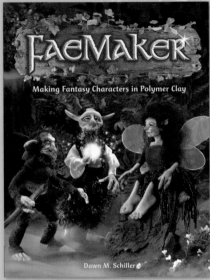